History of
Immigrant Female Students
in Chicago Public Schools,
1900–1950

HISTORY OF
SCHOOLS &
SCHOOLING

Alan R. Sadovnik and Susan F. Semel
General Editors

Vol. 36

PETER LANG
New York • Washington, D.C./Baltimore • Bern
Frankfurt am Main • Berlin • Brussels • Vienna • Oxford

Stephanie Nicole Robinson

History of
Immigrant Female Students
in Chicago Public Schools,
1900–1950

PETER LANG
New York • Washington, D.C./Baltimore • Bern
Frankfurt am Main • Berlin • Brussels • Vienna • Oxford

Library of Congress Cataloging-in-Publication Data

Robinson, Stephanie Nicole.
History of immigrant female students in Chicago public schools,
1900–1950 / Stephanie Nicole Robinson.
p. cm. — (History of schools and schooling; 36)
1. Children of immigrants—Education—Illinois—Chicago—History—20th century.
2. Women immigrants—Education—Illinois—Chicago—History—20th century.
3. Women—Education—Illinois—Chicago—History—20th century.
4. Public schools—Illinois—Chicago—History—20th century.
5. Americanization. I. Title. II. Series.
LC3746.5.I3 R63   371.826'91'09773110904—dc21   2002154419
ISBN 0-8204-6720-0
ISSN 1089-0678

Bibliographic information published by **Die Deutsche Bibliothek**.
Die Deutsche Bibliothek lists this publication in the "Deutsche
Nationalbibliografie"; detailed bibliographic data is available
on the Internet at http://dnb.ddb.de/.

Cover design by Joni Holst

The paper in this book meets the guidelines for permanence and durability
of the Committee on Production Guidelines for Book Longevity
of the Council of Library Resources.

© 2004 Stephanie Nicole Robinson
Peter Lang Publishing, Inc., New York
275 Seventh Avenue, 28th Floor, New York, NY 10001
www.peterlangusa.com

Printed in the United States of America

To Thomas Robinson, Lola Robinson, James Anderson, Ralph Page, William Trent, Violet Harris, Betty Rhodi, Adela Mendez, and Albert Jones

Contents

Tables

CHAPTER 1

Introduction

This is a story about female immigrant students in Chicago's public schools from the era 1900 to 1950. It is told from the perspective of Irish, Polish, Italian, and Jewish immigrant women and girls. Their story is a reflection of wider struggles about immigration, such as assimilation, the retention of ethnic identity, and the way in which public schools were used to mediate crises over diversity.

The negotiation of power in ethnicity, culture, and language occurs in the daily workings of schools. Schools are also one of the places in which naturalized citizens, natural-born citizens, and newcomers regularly interact. Although students spend the greater part of their day in school, they still go home to their immigrant families in their respective immigrant communities. For some students, the lessons learned in school create a source of conflict within the home. Chicago, with its urban setting and its ethnically diverse yet segregated population, was a good place to study how all this plays out.

Although there are many books on immigrant history, few focus exclusively on the schooling experiences of immigrant females. Moreover, the books that are written focus on class, politics, or ethnic differences in schooling. Gender and its underlying issues are not adequately addressed. For example, immigrant women faced hardships due to child-rearing responsibilities, which sometimes resulted in low rates of enrollment and high rates of absenteeism in Americanization classes offered by the Chicago Board of Education.

Moreover, America's societal practice of privileging white males impacted immigrant females in ways that did not affect immigrant men. Immigration laws and Social Security laws enforced these practices. Tensions also existed in the workplace for immigrant women that immigrant men generally did not face, such as sexual harassment.

In addition, traditional cultural expectations placed upon young immigrant females affected their adaptation to American life. Gender role expectations, including preparation for motherhood and marriage, limited the amount of schooling for some girls. Familial obligation such as the care of siblings or a sick parent fell upon girls, hindering them from attending school. While at school, immigrant girls were taught American habits in Little Mothers' classes, which were sometimes at odds with the housekeeping and grooming practices that their mothers taught them at home. Some immigrant girls were also subjected to ridicule by other children because of their clothing and physical appearances. They were expected to conform to American standards of beauty, which at times conflicted with their traditional cultural notions of beauty.

Many historians assumed that when they were writing about men, they were automatically writing about women; that, in fact, "the concerns and interests of women were identical with those of men."[1] They also assumed that when they collected data on the educational experiences of immigrant men, they were automatically including women.[2] The few historians who did include information about immigrant women did not write more than a sentence or two or a paragraph at most on the educational experiences and beliefs of women.[3] Therefore, the focus of most educational historians was ethnic differences among immigrant men regarding their experiences and cultural beliefs about education.[4]

Adding immigrant women's beliefs and educational experiences to history alters previous interpretations that emphasized differences among ethic groups. The result is a history that acknowledges the shared beliefs among cultures regarding the education of women and girls and recognizes the similarities in the educational experiences of immigrant women from different ethnic groups. Furthermore, it shows that parental beliefs regarding the nature and purpose of education vary according to the gender of the children.

Historians also assumed that the Irish, Italian, and Polish immigrants had no cultural traditions that would have encouraged education, while Jewish culture placed a high value on learning. In his book, *Ethnic Differences,* Joel Perlmann argued that Irish culture "would not have encouraged schooling as a means toward economic advancement; indeed, it would not have encouraged any means toward such advancement."[5] He also quoted Kerby Miller's description of the Irish as "communal," "dependent," "more prone to accept conditions passively than to take initiatives for change, and more sensitive to the weight of tradition than to innovative possibilities for the future" in order to illustrate his point that Irish culture did not have characteristics that would be conducive to achievement, academic or otherwise.[6]

Although Perlmann did include the date of Miller's description, Kerby Miller was known for his research on Irish culture from 1650 to 1850.[7] During that time, Ireland was under British domination and Irish Catholics were denied schooling in Ireland.[8] Still, Irish rebellions and the presence of hedge schools in which the Irish secretly taught themselves dispute the accusation that they were "more prone to accept conditions passively."[9]

Perlmann also attributes Irish American attitudes toward school to influences in American society such as increased literacy, changes in the classroom, and the job market. These factors can be traced back to traditional Irish society, and they are influenced by gender. Perlmann wrote:

> The trends in rates of Irish literacy offer some support for these descriptions of a changing peasant outlook. Literacy rates in mid-nineteenth-century Ireland were still low, but rising rapidly. The figures for Ireland suggest that the parents in the 1880 sample were part of a cohort about half of whom were literate; the parents in the 1900 sample were part of a cohort three-quarters literate. . . . In 1880, 22% of the Irish immigrant fathers and 37% of the mothers were illiterate; by 1900, only 6% of the fathers and 14% of the mothers were.[10]

Literacy had become part of Irish society before the mid nineteenth century. Charles Townshend indicated in his book, *Ireland: The Twentieth Century,* that a national system of education for primary grades was established in Ireland as early as 1831.[11] By 1870, there were about a million Irish children in 6,800 elementary schools.[12] He also noted a 14 percent rate of illiteracy.[13] These figures indicate that schools were altering the Irish peasant outlook for at least half a century by 1880.

However, Townshend's figures did not take gender into account. He did not show how many of the children attending school in Ireland were girls or how many women were literate. Perlmann's illiteracy statistics demonstrated that girls were not attending schools at the same rate as boys. Because male and female illiteracy rates among Irish immigrants were relatively low, education had become part of Irish heritage for men. It was believed that Irish women did not need to go to school to fulfill their roles as wives and mothers.[14] Moreover, they were considered intellectually inferior to men and therefore not able to benefit from formal education.[15]

Perlmann theorized that literacy acted as a catalyst in changing Irish culture, which would explain Irish immigrant attitudes toward American schools. He wrote:

> Increasing levels of literacy may erode the attitudes characteristic . . . of the older culture directly, by introducing new ideas. Literacy may be particularly relevant to attitudes of parents concerning their children's education. Alternatively, increased literacy may accompany the economic and social transformations that hasten such attitudinal changes.[16]

Although the ability of immigrants to read and write in English aided their assimilation into American society and made immigrant mothers more likely to enforce the lessons taught in American schools within the home, increases in literacy and school attendance did not significantly alter cultural beliefs about the education of girls in Ireland.[17] In fact, traditional cultural beliefs held by Irish parents as well as societal beliefs regarding the expected gender roles of girls were reflected in the Irish schools. As late as the 1950s, Irish women were taught how to be good wives in school, and they were still treated as intellectually inferior to men.[18]

The increase in the number of Irish schoolteachers, which was also related to gender, was given as a factor in Irish immigrant attitudes toward public schools. Perlmann claimed the presence of Irish

American schoolteachers made the public schools more bearable by 1908. He stated:

> Less than 4% of the public school teachers in 1880 were children of Irish immigrants; by 1908, almost a quarter were, and many more must have been granddaughters of the immigrants by then. It is hard to judge whether so many teachers were of Irish background because the increasing political power of the Irish made their appointment possible or simply because, given the city's ethnic composition, Irish girls would in any case have constituted a large fraction of those entering teaching. . . . In short, it is reasonable to suppose that by 1900, the Irish were keeping their children in school longer because by that time they felt more comfortable with the public schools.[19]

Perlmann was writing about Providence and Boston. In Chicago, St. James, a predominantly Irish Catholic girls' high school, required all of its graduates to take the Chicago Normal School Exam.[20] Since tuition was free for any who passed the entrance exam, teaching was a viable career option for Irish American women.[21] The increase in Irish American public school teachers in Chicago was caused by Catholic schools and not because the Irish were keeping their female children in public schools longer.

According to Howard Ralph Weisz's book, *Irish-American and Italian-American Educational Views and Activities*, the Irish were at odds with sending their children, especially the girls, to Chicago public schools.[22] At the end of the nineteenth century, Irish Catholics were against Protestantism and the pro-British attitudes in the American public schools.[23] Catholic elites such as John Talbot Smith, a newspaper owner, were against tax-supported high schools; he stated that it killed the incentive of the talented few.[24]

Weisz maintained that concerns over health, virtue, and relevancy kept Irish girls out of public schools in the 1890s. He wrote that Irish leaders believed that the failure of the mental and physical health of girls was caused by overstudying in the "blessed public school system."[25] Coeducation in the public schools was linked to prostitution and other societal ills.[26] The public school curriculum was also criticized by an Irish priest in 1903, who stated that "neither literature nor science would prepare a girl for her duties in life."[27]

Similar arguments by Perlmann and Leonard Covello emphasized the lack of intellectual tradition among Italians.[28] In fact, in his book, *The Social Background of the Italo-American School Child*, Leonard Covello argued that Southern Italians did not see any value in attending American schools because they were expected to learn from their parents. He wrote:

> All practical arts and skills should be acquired at an early age by work-ing either in the parental household or through apprenticeship. Knowledge beyond the every-day requirements was a privilege and ne-cessity for the "better" classes.[29]

There were Italian immigrant accounts that confirmed Covello's findings. Excerpts from Thomas Kessner's book, *The Golden Door: Italian and Jewish Immigrant Mobility in New York City 1880–1915*, underscored the point that only the son of the nobility could aspire to obtain enough formal education for a white-collar profession such as a writer.[30] He also wrote, "For girls especially, school was considered superfluous. They were expected to stay home and learn from their mothers." [31] In the 1930s, Therese Giannetti, an Italian American from Chicago, recalled that she went to high school against her parents' wishes.[32]

There was also evidence that showed that all Italian parents did not share this belief. Italian Chicagoan Rosamond Mirabella, born in 1886, stated, "Our people believed in learning. . . . Our people re-spect and like learning."[33] She believed that because Southern Ital-ians were deprived of education in their homeland, they valued the opportunity to obtain it in America.[34] Another Italian Chicagoan, Dante A. Greco, who attended high school in the 1940s, stated that his father was determined to give both him and his sister an educa-tion.[35] Moreover, historian Humbert S. Nelli's book, *From Immi-grants to Ethnics: The Italian Americans*, advanced the view that Italian parents expressed aversion to formal schooling in Italy, but were more willing to send their children to school in America.[36]

Nevertheless, there was more evidence supporting the assertion that Italian parents were against sending their daughters to public schools in America for reasons similar to those expressed by Irish American parents. For example, some Italian Americans also thought that the subject matter taught in public schools was irrelevant.[37] Covello wrote that some Italian American parents, like Irish American parents, believed that attending public schools weakened the morals of children.[38] Immigrant accounts showed that they were especially concerned with protecting the virtue of their female children. One parent expressed the opinion, "Why should she learn to write, she'd only write to her fellas."[39] Dominic Pandolfi, an Italian immigrant who attended high school in the 1920s, remembered that "Italians were very protective about their daughters. It was just unheard of to send her [his sister] off to go two miles to high school and a mixed education."[40]

Historians also wrote that the introduction of foreign values and the desire for child labor influenced Italian immigrant parents against prolonged schooling. Covello wrote that parents expressed fears that the public schools would teach their children new American ideas that were incompatible with their own desire to preserve their cultural traditions.[41] According to reports by the Chicago Board of Education from the 1911–1912 and 1917–1918 school years, these fears were not unfounded. The reports stated that schools were attempting to "break down national customs" through the use of Little Mothers' classes offered to female immigrant students.[42]

The need for child labor was also listed by historians as a reason Italian Americans discouraged children from attending school beyond the elementary level. Nelli cited a 1919 survey stating that 91 percent of Italian American girls fourteen years of age and older living in New York worked for wages.[43] Perlmann suggested that poverty was more prevalent among Italian Americans than among other immigrants and that this was the reason so many of them sent their children to work instead of to high school.[44] Kessner's interpretation agreed with Perlmann. He wrote:

> As a child approaches maturity . . . the parental demands upon the allegiance of the child in his economic role are made in no mistakable terms. . . . The progress of schooling receives, at best, only secondary consideration.[45]

Accounts from immigrant women showed that extenuating circumstances such as parental illness and the expectation of early marriage also prevented girls from continuing to high school.[46] The girls themselves were committed to finishing their education.

Florence Rosetti, for example, dropped in and out of school because her father was ill and then she got married.[47] Eventually, she graduated college and earned a master's degree when she was more than fifty years old.[48] Education was a lifelong pursuit for Italian American women like Florence.

Historians also contended that Polish immigrants, like Irish and Italian immigrants, did not have a culture of learning. Dorota Praszalowicz's article, "The Cultural Changes of Polish-American Parochial Schools in Milwaukee, 1866–1988," implied that they did not have exposure to education in Poland.[49] She wrote:

> In comparison to the old immigration, e.g., Germans, they lacked both skills and financial means at the time of their arrival. . . . Despite the lack of education, their social mobility between 1880–1905 was steady.[50]

Other research supported Praszalowicz's assertions. Irwin T. Sanders and Ewa T. Morawska, in *Polish-American Community Life: A Survey of Research*, cited statistics indicating that 35.5 percent of immigrant Poles were illiterate in the period 1899–1910.[51] They also found that in 1930 the U.S. Census estimated the rate of illiteracy among Polish Americans at 18.5 percent.[52] Although these statistics are not gender specific, Sanders and Morawska did include a study that discovered that in Detroit during the late 1930s, more than half of second-generation Polish women had more schooling than their husbands, a condition that did not exist in the first generation.[53]

Praszalowicz attributed varying levels of education among Polish immigrants to the partitioning of Poland during World War I. She maintained that Polish immigrants from the Prussian partition zone were better educated than immigrants from the Russian and Austrian partition zones, where the "percentage of illiteracy was very high, and the quality of education was much poorer."[54]

However, Helena Znaniecka Lopato in her book, *Polish Americans*, reasoned that differences in parental attitudes toward formal schooling were caused by social class distinctions that existed in Poland before World War I.[55] She wrote:

> Although the upper classes idealized education as a necessary background of the "cultured man," the peasant classes did not adopt this

idealization of education. This anti-intellectualism is evident in the labeling of a person engaged in reading as a deviant, rather than a wise man.[56]

Neither Praszalowicz nor Lopato addressed the issue of gender in their research. In fact, Lopato used research on men to generalize that Polish peasants had negative attitudes toward education. When Victoria Majerski, an immigrant from Austria-dominated Poland, mentioned reasons why she did not attend school in 1907, she did not list politics of the government nor did she mention social class distinctions. She gave the same reason as Irish and Italian immigrant women did for not being educated: she was expected to stay home to help her mother. She said, "I was only eight years old and my brother was only one year old. I take care of him when my mother went to work. That's why I get no school."[57]

Praszalowicz also argued that Polish immigrants were willing to educate their children in America but not in the public schools because of the lack of moral guidance in public school and the immigrant parents' desire to preserve traditional Polish culture.[58] She gave the following reasons to support her argument: parents raised funds to build schools in all nineteen Roman Catholic parishes in Milwaukee, and the number of pupils attending the first school increased from twelve to one hundred within a year.[59]

She also contended that economic conditions created by the Great Depression caused Polish parents to enroll children into the public schools.[60] Immigrant accounts confirmed that the Great Depression was a reason for sending children to public schools or pulling them out of school. Mary Janka, for example, remembered that she had to end her high school career early. She said:

> You must remember that I graduated in the peak of the Depression . . . from grammar school. . . . [My father] felt bad because he couldn't send me to a four course in high school.[61]

In 1935, Virginia Martell said that she had to enroll in public school because "I was no longer able to go to Catholic school because that required too much money."[62]

Lopato and John Bodnar's "Schooling and the Slavic-American Family, 1900–1940" supported the view that Polish immigrants did not value education for women.[63] Lopato wrote that "schooling beyond the requirement set by law was particularly rejected for women"—a rejection based on the belief that "a girl does not 'need' much education."[64] In addition, Bodnar used accounts taken in 1929 from Polish immigrant girls in Nanticoke, Pennsylvania, that indicated that they were taken out of school because their parents wanted their help at home.[65] Moreover, he found that parents believed that their daughters would be best prepared for their future roles as wives and mothers by serving as helpmates to their mothers.[66] He found one father who remarked that a girl does not need schooling "to change diapers."[67] This view was also shared by a Polish immigrant mother in Chicago who complained that her daughter "leaves the housework for me to do and sits and reads a book."[68]

Finally, historical scholarship emphasized that Russian Jewish immigrants had a culture of learning and enthusiastically sent their children to American public schools. Kessner's work, for example, used 1908 studies on the rate of retardation among New York schoolchildren to demonstrate that Jewish commitment to education was higher than other ethnic groups such as Italians. He found that 23 percent of Russian children were left back one year in 1908. Yet the rate of retardation among Italians was not that much higher at 36 percent.[69] He did not list the percentages according to gender.

Kessner also wrote that Jewish commitment to education stemmed from a "non-peasant experience in Europe and by a cultural ideal that respected academic learning."[70] However, some Jews were peasants in Europe. Jewish immigrant women from Russia stated that the distance from their homes to big cities such as Kiev was a factor in whether the possibility of going to school even existed. Anuta Sharrow wrote:

> There in the little towns, Jewish women were limited. There were no schools. . . . Only those that went to school in a big city like Kiev had a chance. In [small] towns, they were locked up at home with housework.[71]

When there were schools nearby, the majority of the Russian population could not afford to send their children to school past the elementary level.[72]

Jewish girls in Poland were also at a disadvantage. Only 17 percent of Jewish girls attended public elementary school in 1906.[73] Eighty percent of the Jewish population in Poland could not send their children to secondary school in 1906.[74]

Moreover, the Jewish tradition of learning was exclusive to the males of the culture. In the early twentieth century, the highly valued role of talmudic scholar, which required lengthy academic preparation, was restricted to Jewish males.[75] As a result, boys, whenever possible, were encouraged to continue in their formal studies.[76] Girls remained home so that they could prepare for their roles as wife and mother by helping their mothers.[77]

Still, Kessner maintained that Jews in America had greater economic security. As result, they "could afford to keep their children in school longer, something they wanted to do anyway."[78] Kessner referred to the presence of Jewish students at City College in New York and a 1910 survey of New York's slums that found more Jews above age sixteen still in school than any other ethnic group to illustrate his points.[79] Here again there was no information given regarding the school enrollment of Jewish female students.

Perlmann cited statistics on Russian Jews in Providence, Rhode Island, to show that Jewish boys and girls were entering and graduating high school at about the same rate. He found that in 1915, 54.3 percent of Jewish boys and 47.5 percent of Jewish girls entered high school.[80] The graduation rate was 21.9 percent for Jewish boys and 21.3 percent for Jewish girls.[81] Although Jewish girls in Providence were graduating high school at about the same rate as boys, they were not given the same type of education, nor were they being educated for the same purpose as Jewish boys. The percentage of Jewish boys enrolled in college prep courses was 44.6 percent, while for Jewish girls it was 6.7 percent.[82]

Economic status was not the only factor determining the length of schooling for Jewish students. Gender also played a part. In Chicago, Jews had scholarship funds for those who could not afford to keep children in school, yet parents still discouraged girls from going to school.[83] For example, in 1914, Mollie Linker, a Jewish immigrant, was put in high fifth in less than two months in school, but she was forced to quit because her father found a job for her.[84]

Abraham J. Karp's book, *Golden Door to America: The Jewish Immigrant Experience,* and Stephan F. Brumberg's book, *Going to America, Going to School: The Jewish Immigrant Public School Encounter in Turn-of-the-Century New York City,* put forth the idea that opportunities for economic advancement and social mobility shaped Jewish attitudes toward education in America.[85] Karp wrote:

> [Jewish] children (including daughters when they could be spared from piece work or housework) took to public school and college with a passion; these institutions for Americanization were the vehicle to economic opportunity and social status.[86]

Accounts from immigrant female students reflected the desire to go to school, but also that they were not spared from housework nor able to effectively use public schools as vehicles to advance themselves. During the early part of the twentieth century, attendance rates for immigrant women in Americanization classes were low. Women were attending these classes at half the rate of men.[87] Fannie Shapiro said that she was so tired after washing diapers and dishes all day that she used to fall asleep in night school.[88] Another female Jewish student, who attended public schools during the day, was discouraged by her mother from excelling in her studies. Her mother stated that "success in school was taboo for women."[89] Finally in 1924, the father of fifteen-year-old Janet Sommers discouraged her from continuing her high school education because he thought she was old enough to work to support herself.[90]

In conclusion, Irish, Italian, Polish, and Jewish immigrant parents shared common beliefs regarding the nature of women's roles and how education should be used to prepare girls for their roles in life as wives and mothers. After inserting data on immigrant women into the research collected on immigrant men, it is clear that ethnic differences regarding the tradition of learning and parental beliefs about schooling in America only applied to immigrant males attending public schools. Immigrant parents expected girls to stay at home and learn from their mothers.

However, accounts from immigrant female students indicated that they wanted to attend school and that they valued education. Still, traditional cultural roles regarding gender and parental expectations hindered most female immigrant students from using the public schools in America for economic gain, social advancement, as vehicles of Americanization, or to educate themselves for purposes of self-development.

Four major themes presented themselves in the stories of Irish, Italian, Polish, and Jewish female immigrants. First and foremost, the Americanization experiences of immigrant women are different from those of immigrant men. Second, accounts from female immigrant students from 1900 to 1950 indicate that Chicago's public schools did not adequately address their cultural beliefs and practices regarding the nature and purpose of education for female children. Third, Americanization/assimilation programs were rendered ineffective because of parental resistance, which manifested itself in truancy and in enrollment in Catholic schools. Fourth, parental beliefs and attitudes toward the education of their children are gender based and culturally rooted in their native homelands.

Chapter 2 concentrates on the Chicago Board of Education's efforts to Americanize immigrant women. Cultural beliefs, the benefits and limitations of citizenship, and hardships faced by immigrant women are also discussed. Although the words "Americanization" and "assimilation" are often used interchangeably by the board and previously written histories, accounts by immigrant women indicate that they are not synonymous. Immigrant women perceived Americanization as public acts made in compliance with the laws and accepted standards of behavior as defined by the dominant American culture. For immigrant women, the act of assimilation meant identifying themselves as Americans and thus passing on the dominant American culture to their children as opposed to their native cultures.

Chapter 3 looks at the Americanization experiences of immigrant students and children of immigrants. Conflicts that occurred between immigrant parents and children and the role of Catholic schools in preserving culture are major themes in this chapter. Other themes include conflicts between the cultural practices of immigrant students and the practices and policies implemented by the Chicago Board of Education and the impact of nativism on immigrant students' efforts to assimilate.

Chapter 4 examines Jewish, Italian, Polish, and Irish immigrant student experiences and attitudes toward school. It compares and contrasts experiences in their native lands with their experiences in

American public schools. It also compares and contrasts parental and student expectations of school. Factors that shape attitudes toward education and schooling experiences, such as gender, class, religion, political climate, and availability of schools, are analyzed. The book ends with a discussion of cultural deficit theory in light of the findings from this study.

Chapters 2, 3, and 4 rely heavily on individual accounts of immigrant women. There are not enough of them to draw general conclusions about each immigrant group as a whole. However, there is merit in discovering heterogeneity within an ethnic group. There were enough accounts to demonstrate differences within a group and to challenge traditional beliefs about the attitudes of ethnic groups toward education. For example, the belief that in the early twentieth century Jews valued education while Italians and Poles did not is redefined and made more complex when gender is interwoven into the class and political dimensions of immigrant schooling.

Although the narrative excerpts and various quotes used throughout are provocative, they present questions about validity. The Scholarship and Guidance Association and United Charity case histories were dependent on the accurate reporting of social workers. Social workers are not journalists. They are trained to record enough information to assess a situation and determine a course of action. The book also highlights problems that occur when social workers are not familiar with the cultural customs of the people they are helping.

Because the autobiographies and oral histories were recorded decades after the events described occurred, there were no accounts from witnesses and corroborating evidence available to verify the women's stories. Still, there was a remarkable amount of consistency in the accounts. Women within the same ethnic groups reported similar experiences. Women from different ethnic groups also reported similar experiences. Because the autobiographies were written and the oral histories were conducted in isolation and yet similarities existed in their reported schooling experiences, differences among the parental attitudes toward the education of their daughters and the schooling experiences of females from different ethnic cultures must be less varied than the differences among men.

CHAPTER 2

Americanization and Immigrant Women

More than eight million immigrants entered the United States between the years 1900 and 1910.[1] Of those immigrants, 158,565 settled in Chicago.[2] The Chicago Board of Education responded to the increase in the city's immigrant population by instituting Americanization programs for adults and children. However, the board's efforts to assimilate immigrant women were at times hostile toward them and ineffective because of low enrollment, lack of attendance, and the importance of religious law in their lives.

The Chicago Board of Education offered three types of Americanization classes for adult immigrants: Mothers' classes, factory classes, and night school classes as well as community center schooling.[3] The classes primarily taught English, although the night school program offered a variety of courses including citizenship classes and vocational skills training.[4] There was evidence that some immigrant women who enrolled in these programs experienced hostility.

Some factory classes were taught on the employer's time during the afternoon or just before closing time.[5] Immigrant factory workers taking those classes were sometimes threatened by their employers. In 1905, the superintendent of Illinois Steel threatened to fire all Slavic workers because they were not learning English fast enough.[6]

In the night school classes, some students were subjected to an abusive examiner. In the early 1900s, Judith Cassai, a tutor, overheard an examiner screaming at a Polish woman in his class. She stated:

> He was hollerin' his head off. Well my people got scared . . . I got in and explained to the man [the difficulties of learning English and becoming an American]. He said, "Did you hear me holler?" I said, "Yes." I said, "What's wrong?" I said, "You've got my students out there scared stiff. They just wish they don't get you." He says, "I hollered to that woman 'cause this is the third time she's coming here [to take the citizenship exam]. And, you know, she won't go to school. She gives me one excuse on top of another. Well, before . . . when she . . . before she gets her citizenship paper, she's gonna have grey hair."[7]

Attendance was a problem for immigrant women and men. The Americanization classes were not very effective in assimilating immigrants because of low rates of enrollment and lack of attendance. In 1920, only 25,000 out of 300,000 unnaturalized immigrants in Chicago enrolled in Americanization classes.[8] There were twenty Mothers' classes in 1920 with an average enrollment of twenty students per class, but only an average of twelve women attended each class.[9] Attendance was better in the factory classes in 1920, but the majority of the students enrolled were men.[10] There were sixty factory classes, with an average enrollment of twenty-five students each and an average attendance of twenty each.[11]

There were no data available on the total enrollment and attendance of immigrant students in all of the thirty-one night school classes offered in 1920.[12] Past enrollment data in English for the foreign-born, a night school class, indicated that more males than females signed up for this class during the 1917–1918 and the 1918–1919 school years. The Americanization survey and accounts taken from immigrants demonstrate that attendance in night school was a problem for working immigrants because of classroom conditions and household responsibilities.

According to Chicago school census data taken during the 1918–1919 school year, the total number of women and men enrolled in Chicago's evening schools was nearly equal. There were 13,468 women and 13,749 men, but these figures do not indicate the number of women and men who were immigrants.[13] Data taken from the enrollment of students in classes for the foreign-born show that the number of female students enrolled was less than half that of their male counterparts. There were 2,154 immigrant men and 896 immigrant women enrolled during the 1918–1919 school year.[14] (See Table 1.)

Moreover, classroom conditions were not favorable to immigrants. Frank Loomis, who conducted the 1920 Americanization in Chicago survey, commented:

> There are no figures to indicate how many foreign born are actually reached or how effectively. It can only be remarked, from the general experience of Americanization workers, that a full-grown adult who has worked at physical labor all day, will not learn much after dinner at night, cramped up in a child's desk in a poorly lighted school room.[15]

There were also language barriers between teachers and students in night school. Judith Cassai explained that she became a tutor because immigrant students did not communicate with the teacher. She said:

> I had to tutor the first new Italians that came, [who were] sent [for] by [their] brothers or fathers. I happened to go to Chicago [and] I taught 'em. I tutored 'em because I used to feel sorry for them. And they had a teacher at the high school, but she could only speak English. She couldn't interpret.[16]

Moreover, attending night school was especially hard for immigrant mothers, who had to work during the day, because they were also responsible for doing household chores and caring for children. Mollie Linker, a Jewish immigrant, who dropped out of school in 1914 in order to work at the age of 13, stated:

> And my regret, I always regret. I should have gone back to school, and I should have kept up. But then, I got married young and I shackled myself to the store. Then, the babies come.[17]

Another Jewish immigrant, Fannie Shapiro, who immigrated in the early twentieth century, recalled how hard it was for her to attend night school:

TABLE 1: Enrollment in Evening Classes for the
Foreign-Born, 1918–1919

Ethnicity	Male	Female	Total
Armenian	10	1	11
Austrian	148	74	222
Belgian	6	4	10
Bohemian	202	124	326
Canadian	4	0	4
Chinese	6	0	6
Cuban	3	0	3
Croatian	68	5	73
Czecho-Slovak	3	5	8
Danish	18	15	33
Egyptian	0	1	1
English	5	1	6
Finnish	11	5	16
French	4	5	9
German	90	70	160
Greek	89	3	92
Holland	7	4	11
Hungarian	53	45	98
Irish	3	2	5
Italian	328	48	376
Japanese	7	0	7
Lithuanian	83	25	108
Mexican	30	5	35
Norwegian	22	23	45
Persian	15	0	15
Polish	453	151	604
Roumanian	6	10	16
Russian	295	174	469
Scotch	1	0	1
Servian	31	1	32
Slavic	30	11	41
S. American	4	1	5
Spanish	21	4	25
Swedish	90	76	166
Turkish	2	0	2
Ukrainian	1	0	1
Total	2154	896	3,050

Source: Annual Report of the General Superintendent of the
Chicago Public Schools, 1918–1919.

When I came home from night school, I was so tired. After all, I'd fall asleep there. So I had to give it up. I went and bought one of those translators and I used to [learn with it], after washing all the diapers and all the dishes and going to bed and getting up.[18]

In fact, night school attendance was so poor that factory classes at companies such as National Malleable Casting were instituted to take their place.[19]

Still, immigrant women who were able to successfully complete Americanization courses by becoming citizens and gaining mastery of the English language were protected against circumstances that women who were not citizens sometimes encountered. However, they were denied certain citizenship privileges that were granted to immigrant men because they were women. Moreover, for some immigrant women, religious laws and traditional customs took precedence over public laws and American customs, especially in matters concerning their families. For those women, the benefits derived from becoming American were limited to the public sphere. In this way, they were also able to regulate the assimilation of their children.

Immigrant women, although they had become citizens, were denied privileges that were granted to male citizens. For example, they were not able to file a petition for the immigration of their female relatives, including their own daughters. According to the Immigration Laws of 1917 and 1924, a woman was not able to immigrate without a petition from a male citizen or resident alien.[20] A female citizen could not initiate a petition. After a woman obtained a petition from a male citizen, she had to be met at the port by a spouse or a male relative.[21]

There were other laws that disenfranchised female citizens, such as those pertaining to social security. A single woman could not collect Social Security benefits upon retirement.[22] This forced women to stay married or to remarry. One Jewish woman, who was married three times, described her experiences:

I got to know in one of the shops, a woman, a friend. And she had a brother who was divorced. And she started talking me into marrying her brother. And I didn't want to get married, but it was hard for me to work for a living in the factory. I didn't care too much for him. But about two or three years later, I married this man. Otherwise, I couldn't have got Social Security.[23]

American women also faced problems when they married men from overseas. In the 1920s, one American woman faced expatriation for being married to a foreign spouse. The eighteen-year-old woman went to Ireland to marry. After the marriage went sour, she found that she had waited too long to apply for readmission into the United States and lost her citizenship status.[24]

In the workplace, male bosses had total control over their female employees. Although laws were passed to protect women, they were not enforced. Bosses could refuse to allow women to use the restroom. [25] Some employers required workers to stand twelve or more hours even though state laws required seats for women. When the larger stores supplied chairs in compliance with the law, managers fired women who sat down.[26]

Immigrant women were also subjected to sexual harassment, which was generally not a problem for immigrant men. Those who refused their bosses' advances were fired. In 1926, Maud Nathan wrote:

> Floorwalkers in the old days were veritable tsars; they often ruled with a rod of iron. Only the girls who were "free-and-easy" with them, who consented to lunch or dine with them, who permitted certain liberties, were allowed any freedom of action or felt secure in their positions.[27]

Fannie Shapiro also recalled an incident that happened to her while at work. She stated:

> One day the machine, those old machines, broke. I had to get up on the table to reach it. So when I went up on the table reaching and the boss, an old man, he went and pinched me so I gave him a crack and he fell. He was very embarrassed. So the whole shop went roaring. He thought I would keep quiet. I was so naive. I thought a man touched me. . . . So he fired me. He told me, "Get out, greenhorn." He was right, not I.[28]

Non-English-speaking women were the most vulnerable. They could not defend themselves or effectively seek help until they learned English. Rosa Cohen, a Jewish immigrant, worked in the New York garment district at age twelve and was continually molested by her boss. After she became bilingual, she recalled that her first English sentence was "Keep your hands off please."[29]

Although immigrant female citizens were subjected to injustices not faced by immigrant males, they had no more rights than noncitizens. Women lived under the threat of deportation and were more susceptible to abuse. Immigrant women's status in the United States was not secure because legislation limited their rights. The Immigration Laws of 1917 and 1924 stated that a petition could be withdrawn at will.[30] Only a spouse or citizen could appeal a denial of a petition.[31]

There was a case in the 1920s involving a German immigrant woman whose husband refused to receive her. After he sent for her, he wrote her a letter telling her that he changed his mind about her coming to America. He claimed that he wanted their son to be educated in Germany. She arrived in America before the letter got to Germany. Upon her arrival, she discovered that her husband was having an affair with a woman at the boardinghouse where he was staying. He intended to let her be deported. In this scenario, she and her son would have become homeless and destitute—since she did not speak English and would have had a hard time finding employment—eventually becoming a ward of the state. Luckily, the United Charities intervened and found housing and employment for the woman and her son.[32]

Sometimes a woman did not even get to the port because her husband refused to file a petition for her to immigrate. A Jewish woman related:

> It would happen to me the same thing as happened to others if you did have a hundred dollars. You got married, [he] took the money, and he left you right away [for] America. Sometimes he sent for you. Sometimes he found someone he liked better and forgot you. Sent you a divorce [instead of a ticket].[33]

Once a woman arrived and was received, she was still vulnerable to abuse. As a newcomer, she was dependent on her husband and was unlikely to be familiar with the legal system, her legal rights, social service agencies, or medical care services.[34] For example, in the 1920s, there was an Armenian woman whose husband did not get along with her elderly immigrant parents. He took their money to buy an estate for himself, leaving them penniless. Since they could not speak English or find work, they asked to be deported.[35] Because the woman's parents were not citizens, they had little or no rights.

In another example of abuse, a husband took advantage of his immigrant wife's inability to speak English. In the 1930 United Charities Annual Report, a caseworker claimed that she had saved their marriage. The Americanized husband claimed that he was ashamed of his wife's Old World ways. He also said that his wife nagged him about having casual conversation with other women.[36]

In reality, he was having affairs. His wife's inability to speak English allowed him to do this in front of her. However, she recognized that he was flirting with other women in front of her and complained to a caseworker from United Charities. The caseworker's solution was to teach her how to dress better and offer her English instruction.[37] The caseworker explained to her that women had more freedom in America and that it was okay to have conversations with men.[38]

Americanization did not guarantee that a husband would mend his ways, but it was used to justify his behavior. He received no counseling to suggest ways to make his wife feel more comfortable. Instead, the woman was blamed for not making herself more attractive to her husband.

During the Depression, another woman, Carmella Zoppettiti, ended her marriage because of her husband's alcoholism. She was Americanized and able to survive on her own because of her knowledge and willingness to accept American institutions. She said:

> I went to the social service and they told me what to do for it. I didn't even know how to get him out of the house. I got the check. And I've been on my own ever since. And today I am on my own and I'm well provided . . . all by myself, not by him. I am 100%. . . . Now I can live in peace and I know I have something. But if I was with him, I would just be working as a mother . . . bearing children, bringing unnecessary children into this world.[39]

Despite the protection that American laws offered its citizens, some immigrant women believed that religious law had more authority. They maintained their beliefs even at the expense of their rights as American citizens. Kataya Govsky, who was married at age twenty-six, described her situation thus:

> I was married for two years. I had a son in 1931, and my happiness was unlimited but it didn't last too long. My husband was transferred to New York, and when he got to New York, there was no job because

of the Depression. . . . [One day,] my husband's uncle comes and tells me he's married. I wanted a divorce. My womanly pride was stronger than my feelings toward him, and I didn't want him. I went to the criminal court and the man said, "In twenty-four hours, you can get a divorce." And that's what happened, but Pa says, "You have to get a Jewish divorce."[40]

A divorce granted by a judge was not considered a true divorce. Because the marriage took place in a church, it was subject to the laws of religion. A divorce had to be granted by the faith. Kataya continued, "It took a year with all the investigations. I wanted to adopt my son. You know a child belongs to the father."[41] A rabbi had to go to New York to talk with her husband and fill out papers. Then four rabbis questioned her and had her repeat ceremonial words.[42] They told her to bury her papers. Then they said, "You're clean again. You can remarry."[43]

The procedure made Kataya feel as though she had done something wrong. She had to adopt the children that she bore. She was interrogated, although her husband was the bigamist. She was "unclean" because she had sexual relations with her own husband.

There is evidence that these practices changed over time. Another Jewish woman during World War II was able to free herself from a bad marriage because job opportunities allowed her financial independence. Moreover, she accepted the authority of American laws, which allowed her to divorce her husband and claim her son more expediently than Kataya Govsky did. She said:

He's not trying anything. I was making then already more than he did. I told him, "I want to break up with you," and I did. I divorced him and I took my boy with me.[44]

Another practice, domestic abuse, was not really considered abuse but punishment for not being a good wife. It was culturally accepted behavior and supported by the family. A woman who lived in both Italy and America revealed the following:

As a young wife, I was no angel. I was obstinate and revolted against my husband, whose ideas seemed to me crazy. I was made stronger than he. Whenever he tried to hit me, I was ready to hit him back. That was in our home. But he had it on me for he fixed me many a time on the street. There on the street, I didn't even think of resisting him. If I did that, I certainly would disgrace him. . . .[45]

However, when the same woman immigrated to America, she found out that being hit by her husband was not an acceptable practice in American culture. She persisted in her beliefs, although she was taunted by American women. She stated:

> Once he gave me a "lantern" [a black eye]. I nursed the sore spot at home day and night, and wore a kind of bandage around the eye. But I can remember that whenever I went to the street I went without the bandage. And as I remember now, I didn't feel any shame. Nobody made nasty cracks at me as they would do here in America.[46]

Another Italian immigrant, Rose Tellerino, who arrived in Chicago in 1900 at the age of one, was told by her mother to drop out of school at age fourteen. She was supposed to get married that year to a barber, who was twenty-four. When he beat her up, her mother took his side. Rose reported:

> I lived with him but it was not my match. I was just a child. I still wanted to act like a child. . . . He was trying to act like a father, naturally. I was still a rebellious child you know and he would hit me. And he would hit me and then I would go to my mother and tell her about it. *Ma marita*, John, I would call him, his name was John but I called him the barber. And she would say, "Ah. You must have done something." You know they never gave the credit to the daughter always the husband.[47]

In all these instances, it was considered the woman's fault that she was beaten by her husband. She had broken the rules and was not offered safe haven. Even women who immigrated as children and lived in America their whole lives complied either willingly or by compulsion with the cultural norms and religious laws of their parents. For those women, Americanization was a public act. It was something that was limited to the public and not necessarily practiced in their homes.

Finally, the Americanization of immigrant women was important because these women ultimately controlled the assimilation of immigrant children in their care. Immigrant mothers decided when and where it was appropriate for their children to be Americans.

For example, Virginia Martell, who was born in 1921 in the United States to immigrant parents from Poland, credited her parents for teaching her English.[48] They learned English and they spoke it in the home. She said:

My parents started to learn the English language while they were in New Jersey. By the time they came to Chicago they knew enough to get by on. My mother later went to the Laird Community House where she studied the English language and she got herself a diploma by going to school there. My father learned the English language as he worked in the butcher shop. He picked it up there.[49]

There were some students who learned English at school but were discouraged from speaking it at home. Dominic Pandolfi, who was born in 1908 to Italian immigrants, recalled his Americanization experiences:

Well, I started my schooling in the public school. Most of the children there were Polish or Italian. Most of them were Italian. We had one or two German children there. The teachers were of course quite concerned about these foreigners and we all wanted to be 100% American. So it was in most of the homes that Italian was spoken but we made an attempt to get our parents to be American because this was out of a feeling of being American.[50]

He was exposed to Americanization at school, but it was not enforced at home. His parents remained Italian speakers and maintained their traditional culture. As a result, he was forced to limit his Americanized behaviors (i.e., speaking English) when he was at home. Based on the statistics given on the number of immigrants enrolled in and attending Americanization programs, this was not an uncommon experience.

Another immigrant, Mary Janka, whose parents were from Poland, had a similar experience in the 1920s.[51] She said that she was taught English in school. She also spoke to her friends in English, although they were Polish too. However, she said that when she was at home, "I always had to converse with my parents in Polish. I think that's one of the reasons I speak it so fluently."[52]

An immigrant mother, Maria Valiani, who was raising her children in the 1920s, gave her views on Americanization, more specifically, learning to speak English.[53] She said:

English, they go to school, they'll always learn. Speak Italian in the house. Then, my little boy came home one day and he said, "You know what the teacher told me, mama? That I shouldn't speak Italian at home because, she said, you don't learn your English." Some teachers are stupid. Some teachers, they do the damage. So I didn't have time to go to the teacher and bawl her out. But I said, "You speak Italian when you're home with Grandma because she don't understand English."[54]

Although Maria Valiani was born in the United States in 1902 and learned to speak English at school, her Italian immigrant mother never learned to speak English, so she had to speak Italian while at home. She continued to speak Italian at home as an adult. Her son also learned English at school. It was not taught to him as his first language. After he learned English at school, she encouraged him to continue to speak Italian at home because of his grandmother. Ultimately, immigrant mothers, not the public schools, determined whether or not their children would be English-speaking Americans.

Although the Chicago Board of Education used various programs such as Mothers' classes, factory classes, and night school programs to Americanize Chicago's immigrant population, their efforts were for the most part in vain. Only a fraction of the total immigrant population was enrolled in and actually attended these programs because of the difficulties of working and going to school. These problems were compounded for immigrant women, who also had childcare and household duties. For those who did attend Americanization programs, they sometimes experienced a hostile learning environment caused by physically uncomfortable classrooms, language barriers, and abusive teachers. Immigrant women who completed the Americanization programs were more secure in their status than immigrant women who were noncitizens, but they were still subjected to hardships that immigrant men generally did not face. Although some women allowed themselves to be Americanized, they did not give up their culture. Instead, they became Americans in public, but at home maintained their native culture, as evidenced by their adherence to religious laws and their refusal to teach their children to speak English as their first language. Therefore, the success of the Chicago Board of Education's Americanization programs depended on the extent to which they could successfully assimilate immigrant women, who would then raise their children to be Americans.

CHAPTER 3

Americanization Activities in Chicago Public Schools

Beginning in the early 1900s and throughout the 1930s, various special interest groups and politicians vied for control over the curriculum in the Chicago public schools. All sides used Americanization as their platform and claimed to represent the interests of the disenfranchised. On November 7, 1902, the Chicago Teachers Federation joined forces with the Chicago Labor Federation to launch an attack on the major employers' groups in Chicago, who railed against the teaching of music, art, and foreign languages to working-class children.[1] In 1909, the Chicago Association of Commerce had published a report, *Industrial and Commercial Education in Relation to Conditions in the City of Chicago,* in which vocational education was stressed for working-class boys and girls as a means to comply with the "rightful demands of the state" by being "intelligent, moral, and patriotic."[2] In 1927, Chicago's former mayor William (a.k.a. "Big Bill") Thompson won reelection for the third time by capitalizing on the demands of Polish, German, French, Irish, and other ethnic groups for representation in the curriculum and by promising to replace the alleged pro-British textbooks that were adopted by the Chicago Board of Education.[3] He also said that if he was reelected mayor he would "make the schools citadels of sturdy Americanism—a nursery of good citizenship."[4]

The Chicago Board of Education heightened its own Americanization efforts during 1900–1910 when 54,380 immigrant students and 503,006 American-born students with immigrant parents enrolled in Chicago's public schools.[5] Before Thompson first gained political prominence in 1911, the Chicago Board of Education was using the public school system to Americanize immigrant children.[6] Various activities within the public school system were used to build "good American citizenship."[7] Civics classes were used specifically for this purpose.[8] The Committee on Civic Education, a part of the superintendent's Advisory Council of the Chicago Public Schools, listed three objectives of civic training: to provide a thorough understanding of the facts of the historical, economic, and political background of modern culture; to develop a sense of the comparative values of human activities, achievements, and satisfactions and socially desirable habits of choice among all these; to use a technique of instruction to connect the facts of the cultural background with the facts of current experience and open opportunities for rational participation in group life in increasingly larger units.[9]

While these were lofty aspirations to strive toward, they did not reflect what actually took place in the public schools. The study of modern culture was a series of units in American history and local government with very little mention of other cultures. Moreover, American culture was the standard that other cultures were measured against. In fact, accounts taken from immigrant students show that the public schools considered only American habits socially desirable. Furthermore, nativist attitudes and practices within the public schools prevented some immigrant students from participating in the group life of the school. For those students, school was a place marked by isolation and exclusion.

Modern Culture Means American Culture

Although the Chicago Board of Education stated that one of the objectives of civic education was to study the foundations of modern culture, the proposed subject matter in civic education courses, despite Mayor Thompson's efforts, offered little instruction on cultures that were not American, especially after the sixth grade. From kindergarten to the sixth grade, there were only five lessons reserved for the study of non-American cultures. These included stories of simpler civilizations; the life of the people of the countries studied; geography and people of North and South America; and studies of European history, chivalry, discovery, and geography and people of other continents.[10] There was no proposed instruction of other cultures in the seventh and eighth grades and there were two elective courses on European history offered at the high school level. (See Table 2.)

It appeared as though the units devoted to the study of local communities added diversity to the curriculum because Chicago was composed of a variety of ethnic communities. However, a team of

TABLE 2: Subject Materials Most Frequently Used in Civic Courses

Grade	Subject matter
Kindergarten–Third Grade	Projects in home, school, and neighborhood activities (e.g., including postal service)
	Projects to teach safety habits.
	Stories of simpler civilizations.
	Celebrations of anniversaries and holidays (in succeeding grades also).
Fourth–Fifth Grade	Selected stories of American history.
	Geography—types of land areas.
	Life of people of countries studied.
	Some activities of the local community.
Sixth Grade	Stories of colonial American days.
	Stories of European history, chivalry, discovery.
	Geography and people of other countries.
Seventh Grade	American history.
	Transportation and communication in the local community.
	Local history.
Eighth Grade	American history.
	Current events discussions.
	Community civics.
Ninth Grade	American history.
	Structure of national, state, and city government.
	Vocational or economic civics.
Tenth Grade	Early and medieval European history (usually an elective).
Eleventh Grade	Modern European or industrial history (usually an elective).
Twelfth Grade	American History—1 year required.
	Civic or Problems of Democracy—½ year required.
	Other courses in sociology and economics (elective).

Source: Chicago board of Education, Education for Citizenship, March 1933, Chicago, Illinois.

specialists who investigated the social science courses in 1932 found that the "elementary schools do not make adequate use of the Chicago environment."[11] Moreover, a report made in 1933 by the Committee on Civic Education stated that histories of the local community as well as community resources were "too scanty to offer teachers much help."[12] Some immigrant parents enrolled their children in Catholic schools in response to their histories and cultures being excluded from the public schools.[13] They considered Catholic schools a viable alternative to public schools. When Catholic schools began to seek state accreditation, the government began to pressure them into teaching English, and the desire to demonstrate loyalty to American institutions caused Catholic schools to more closely resemble public schools.

From 1900 to 1930, a reported 55.4 percent of all Catholic school children attended officially ethnic schools and the other 44.6 percent attended Catholic schools that were open to anyone but were predominantly Irish.[14] Catholic schools appealed to immigrants for reasons of culture, language, and national identity—the Polish Catholics attended Polish Catholic schools, the Irish attended Irish Catholic schools, and so on. They also appealed to immigrants by offering language instruction in their native tongues and courses in the history of their homelands.[15]

In 1925, St. Philip's, an Italian parochial school, described itself as

the school where your children learn that there does exist in the world a land called Italy, mother of every present civilization and center of Christianity. It is the school where they will not be ashamed of being known as Italians, offspring of saints and heroes. It is the school where they will learn to speak the language of Dante, the sweet and beautiful Italian language.[16]

Other immigrant groups, such as Polish Americans, also sent their children to Catholic schools to preserve their culture. Historian Helena Znaniecka Lopato wrote that Polish parents found American public schools unacceptable in terms of their emphasis on American culture, language, history, and geography, to the exclusion of Polish culture.[17]

Twentieth-century Irish-Catholic schools were exceptional because they taught English. Originally, Irish history was not included in the curriculum.[18] Irish Catholic schools were compelled to teach Irish history because the Ancient Order of Hibernians pushed for its inclusion during an organized campaign in 1904.[19] Because of these exceptions, the English-speaking parochial schools of the Irish had more in common with local public schools than they did with their German or Polish counterparts. While other ethnic groups used parochial schools to preserve and defend ancestral language and customs, the Irish used their schools to promote integration into American society.

In time, Catholic schools began to resemble public schools because of their desire for accreditation and pressure from the government during wartime. As early as the 1890s, St. James, an Irish parish, opened a high school for girls that had similar features to the public schools, such as graded classrooms, teaching institutes, and university extension courses.[20] The curriculum was also patterned after the public school course right down to the same textbooks.[21]

A Polish parish, St. Stanislaus Kostka, opened a two-year commercial school for girls in 1914.[22] Its purpose was to "train young ladies for positions in the business and office areas, as well as to provide an education otherwise available only in public or non-sectarian schools."[23] In 1916, a committee from the Chicago Board of Education visited the school and within two weeks the school was placed on the accredited list of schools in the city of Chicago.[24] By 1934, the two-year commercial school became a two-year high school with accreditation from the State of Illinois in Springfield.[25]

Pressure from the U.S. government during wartime contributed to the changes in the Catholic schools. There was a need for English-speaking soldiers. Helena Znaniecka Lopato wrote:

> Around 1918 the United States government began to pressure Polonia to accept the standardized schedule of classes and to use English in its schools, charging that too many young men in the armed services did not understand or speak English.[26]

Among the many potential problems caused by the lack of effective communication with non-English-speaking soldiers, the most dangerous would probably be the inability to follow orders. This inability could compromise the war effort by endangering the lives of non-English-speaking soldiers as well as their fellow soldiers.

During World War II, some people claimed that the government's push for English only in schools caused the loss of interest in Catholic education and was detrimental to the war effort. For example, Martha Leszcyk, a Polish immigrant, claimed that because of Mrs. Roosevelt's initial criticism of everyone who used a second language, Polish schools discontinued every language except English.[27] She said:

> So, the worst thing was many active groups they were very angry and they were even ready to stop belonging to the Church. Because they said that if we shall get the English language only in our schools, why should we pay for the school, we'll send them to the public school. But then after Mrs. Roosevelt came back [from visiting the troops during the war] it was different. Then you had to learn [another language].[28]

Leszcyk explained that Mrs. Roosevelt influenced government policy during the war without adequately assessing the situation. She stated that after Mrs. Roosevelt observed the conditions, she realized that the English-only policy was hindering the war effort. Leszcyk continued:

> When [Mrs. Roosevelt] went overseas, she saw that the soldiers could not cooperate with foreign soldiers because they could only speak English. Upon her return, she wrote an article saying that every child must learn at least two languages.[29]

The quote also shows how the military's needs changed over time. During World War I, the inability to speak English posed a problem because non-English-speaking soldiers were unable to communicate with other soldiers or their commanding officers. During World War II, the inability to speak a foreign tongue was a problem because English-speaking soldiers could not understand the language of their allies.

Lastly, the desire of Catholic schools and students to demonstrate their acceptance of American institutions and ideals caused Catholic schools to become less ethnic in nature and more comparable to public schools. For example, the *Il Calendario Italiano* declared in 1925 a commitment to promote Americanism in Italian Catholic schools.[30] It stated:

> Far from being a menace to our American institutions . . . our Catholic educational institutions are daily proving themselves the real bul-

warks for our national life, the best conservators of our American ideals, the foundation sources where our future American citizens receive the most thorough preparation for the fulfillment of their religious and civic responsibilities.[31]

The desire for Italian Catholic schools to prove their allegiance to American institutions springs from one of the many attacks that the board had launched against Catholic schools. In 1923, for example, Superintendent William McAndrew stated:

> There is a large number of foreign-born, foreign language-speaking children in the Pope Schools who are unable to carry forward the work in the regular grade classrooms. It is necessary to open for them a special room, in which they may be taught more advantageously.[32]

Within this statement, McAndrew implied that Catholic schools were not American institutions. They belonged to the pope, hence the term "pope schools." Even though Catholic schools were being accredited by the Chicago Board of Education as well as the State of Illinois in Springfield, he maintained the belief that Catholic schools were still academically inferior to public schools.

A weekly Polish newsletter, the *Obronca*, indicated that changes were occurring in the Polish Catholic schools that were contrary to the original intent of schools to promote the study of Polish language and history.[33] It stated:

> The English language is increasingly encroached upon the Polish parish schools. In schools on which Polish people have spent tens of millions of dollars to have their children brought up in a Polish way, you can rarely hear a few everyday Polish words.[34]

According to the *Obronca*, Polish parish schools were not "Polish" anymore. They had become Americanized. Instead of teaching its students Polish culture through the study of Polish language and history, the children were being assimilated in the same way that they would have been in the public schools. It is ironic that ethnic newspapers were complaining that their schools were too much like American public schools, while the Chicago Board of Education's stance was that Catholic schools were not American at all.

Still, the fact remains that Catholic schools were loosening their ethnic ties and becoming institutions where American loyalty was stressed more than ethnic allegiances. Students such as Sam Spirale, a member of the 1926 graduating class at St. Philips, expressed their acceptance of American culture and its institutions.[35] The following is an excerpt from Sam's graduation speech, in which he expressed reverence for the American flag and immigrants who sacrificed to become "true Americans":

> What we always love and respect is our Flag. It stands for Washington and the patient brave struggle he made for our country. It stands for the soldier of Valley Forge whose bare feet left marks of blood on the snow. It stands for the fathers who toiled uncomplainingly to earn food and clothes and a chance for education for their children, and mothers who cook and sew, sacrifice so that their children, may be true Americans. So we leave for you of the next class, the emblem of the brave the Flag and liberty, which represents all the true men and women, boys and girls, who now live in the United States or have ever lived in the United States.[36]

Sam's speech linked the facts of the historical, economic, and political background of American culture to the experiences of immigrant parents in America. The ability of immigrant students to see themselves as part of American cultural heritage led to the loosening of ethnic ties. When Americanization occurred in this way, it did not require the rejection of the immigrants' ethnic pasts because it provided them with an American past.

American Habits Are Socially Desirable

The second objective of civic education mentioned that students would develop socially desirable habits of choice after comparing the norms of different cultures. However, immigrant students in Chicago public schools were not given a choice. They were encouraged to assimilate. They learned that American habits were socially desirable and that American culture was the standard against which their native culture was measured. Moreover, immigrant girls had an added burden: they had to conform to American notions of beauty. The Chicago Board of Education encouraged immigrant children to assimilate by using the public schools to indoctrinate them with American ideals and teach them American customs. Fears of anarchy and treason prevented the board from offering immigrant students the opportunity to choose whether or not to become Americans or a composite of different ethnic cultures possessing various national loyalties.

During the 1900–1901 school year, board president Graham Harris expressed his fears of anarchy and treason, which were more than likely caused by the increase in the foreign-born population in Chicago at this time. He wrote:

> The chief bulwark of American institutions is the public school. As such, it should receive the hearty support of every citizen who has a spark of patriotism in his heart. If our children attend school regularly and are reared in an atmosphere of true Americanism, with a reverence for the flag that floats over the school house, anarchy and assassination will be stamped out, and the names of our future Presidents will not be on a nation's tears.[37]

It should be understood that these fears were shared by American-born people, and thus they would not view the board's intentions to use the public schools to exclusively promote Americanism as an infringement on the rights of immigrants or contradictory to the objectives of civic education.

As late as 1917, social workers Edith Abbott and Sophonisba P. Breckinridge reflected this view when writing about the use of compulsory education laws as a means of safeguarding the city government and the American way of life. They wrote:

> For it should be kept in mind that the institutions of the city are those developed by American experience in the working out of American ideals. The city government may rest for support upon the vote of the German, Irish, or Scandinavian colonies; but the city government is not German, Irish or Scandinavian. The children may speak Polish, Hungarian, Russian or Yiddish; but these same children are to be trained for civic life that has grown out of American experience and Anglo-Saxon tradition, and for an industrial life based on new world ideas of industrial organization.[38]

In regard to protecting America against the threat of anarchy, they wrote:

> If compulsory education laws were needed for the education of the native American, they are doubly needed for the immigrant who today

needs to learn not only our language, but also the principles of our democracy, if these principles are to endure and "the promise of American life" is not to be obscured.[39]

After the outbreak of World War I, the need to ensure that immigrants were loyal and supported American institutions became more urgent. The 1917–1918 Board of Education's Annual Report stated:

> Unfortunately all too large is the fraction of the population of the city that is still foreign, despite the heroic measures which have been taken to imbue them with American ideas and to instill in them a love for American institutions.[40]

Although attempts were made to Americanize immigrants to ensure political loyalty, the board discovered that immigrants did not easily cast off the culture of their native lands. Immigrant students persisted in speaking in their native tongues and practicing their customs despite Americanization efforts. The following statement was taken from the board's 1917–1918 Annual Report. It illustrates the board's intent to assimilate immigrant students as well as its failure to do so.

> But it is a stupendous undertaking to attempt to break down national customs which have become firmly grounded and it is almost futile to seek to supplant the language in which our immigrants were reared, and which they have continued to use in adulthood.[41]

One reason why the board was not very successful in its attempts to "break down national customs" was that some immigrant children entered school with a strong sense of ethnic identity and cultural pride. Margaret Sabella, an Italian American, displayed such characteristics in the recollection of her experiences in the Chicago public schools. She recalled:

> When I started grade school (1920s), I discovered other ethnic groups and had some very close girlfriends, other than the Italian girlfriends. I was interested in their way of life. Their way of life was different than ours. Yes, it was different. I didn't think it was better. I didn't think theirs was better. I thought ours was.[42]

Previous attempts at assimilation included the Little Mothers' classes, which began during the 1911–1912 school year in response to high infant mortality rates.[43] Little Mothers' classes were offered to girls in the higher grades at sixty-four elementary schools.[44] They were more than likely aimed at immigrant girls because those grade levels corresponded with the age range (between twelve and fifteen years old) in which they were most likely to drop out of school in order to get married.[45] The duties of motherhood and the care of children during infancy were taught. Lectures were also given on domestic hygiene and the selection, presentation, and preparation of food. In addition, the need for bodily care and sanitary environment was stressed.[46]

The board found that despite these classes, which taught the selection and preparation of American food, some immigrants still refused American dishes. The initial failure of the Penny Lunch Program was a good case in point. Immigrant students refused to have their eating habits Americanized. The board advised:

> Principals must necessarily cater to local food tastes based upon nationality if the prime purpose of the lunch room is to be achieved—the feeding of the hungry child. One might be last to believe that a hungry child will eat anything that will allay the pangs of hunger, but experience has proven this untrue. No matter how famished, children apparently will eat only those foods they have been in the habit of eating at their homes.[47]

Realizing that immigrant students, no matter how hungry, would not change their diets, the Chicago public schools changed their lunchroom policy during the 1911–1912 school year to better serve them.

However, the board failed to realize that the problem with the Penny Lunch Program was more serious than just the reluctance to try new foods. In some cultures, such as Judaism, food has religious connotations. Jews believe that it is a sin against God to break kosher (dietary) regulations. In the following anecdote, which took place in 1882, a Jewish girl recalled that her mother believed in keeping kosher so strongly that she was willing to let herself and her children go hungry.

> We had to walk a short distance when we saw some bright yellow things that we had never seen before and some shiny red apples. Being of an adventurous nature, my sister decided to try the yellow things. She held up seven fingers and pointed to the bananas, for that's what

they were called, the man told us. When Mother saw what we had brought, she was afraid the things were not kosher. They looked like sausages, and she would not allow us to eat them. After that eventful shopping expedition we had .85 left and we were still hungry.[48]

The board was oblivious to the influence that parents had on their children. The point made in that 1882 anecdote still rang true in 1911. Regardless of circumstances such as intense hunger, parents control what their children will and will not eat. Furthermore, new foods must be approved and/or introduced by parents. The anecdote also attests to this fact within its conclusion. "As the horse clattered over the brick pavements of the station yard, Father opened a brown paper bag and gave each of us a banana."[49] Food that was previously forbidden was now safe to eat because a parent approved it.

When children adopted an American habit learned at school, they were sometimes met with resistance by their parents when they practiced that habit at home. For example, home economics classes and Little Mothers' classes taught immigrant girls lessons in hygiene and grooming practices that some parents found unacceptable. In 1950, there was a German American girl who would constantly argue with her mother about the proper way to wear and care for garments.[50] One of the arguments was over a blouse. Her mother felt that D. should wear her blouse two or three times between washings.[51] D. wanted to wear it once to school and hang it up to wear after school.[52] Her mother insisted that she should wear it more often, even though it was D., rather than her mother, who washed and ironed her blouses.[53] Clearly D.'s mother was concerned with the habits that D. learned at school and not with the prospect of having more laundry to do. This observation was also supported by another incident. D. had another argument with her mother because she hung her soiled clothes on a hanger rather than putting them back in her drawers as her mother had taught her.[54] Again D.'s mother disapproved of D.'s newly acquired American habits.

Moreover, it was just as important for immigrant children to look like Americans as it was for them to think and act like Americans. Proper clothing was so vital that, in 1943, the Service Council for Girls, a case working agency that operated in conjunction with the Juvenile Court and the Compulsory Education Department of the

TABLE 3: Service Council for Girls' Disbursements, 1/28/1943–2/28/1943

Committee	Item	Charge	Contribution	Net
Case	Carfare	$ 26.68		
	Board	27.00		
	Lunch & Rec.	30.64		
	School Supplies	4.53		
	Medical Care	15.00		
	Worker's Expense	10.09		
Total		113.94	6.0	107.94
Clothing	Clothing Articles	8.96		
	Material	35.00		
	Shoes	7.10		
Total		51.06		51.06

Source: Arthur Young and Company, Accountants and Auditors Statement of Disbursements of Case and Clothing Committee.

Board of Education, spent more money purchasing material to make clothes than it did on food.[55] (See Table 3.)

Adequate attire was necessary to prevent poor immigrant students from dropping out of school in order to avoid being teased by other students. John Bodnar also discovered this when he interviewed Slavic Americans who went to school between the years 1900 and 1940.[56] He found that one woman left school at the age of 13 because her coats and dresses were ragged.[57] Another woman dropped out in the third grade because she had no shoes to wear to school.[58] There was a man who refused to leave his neighborhood to attend classes because "Americans had better clothes than we had."[59]

Maria Vallani, who emigrated from Italy in 1911 at the age of nine, was teased, but she thought her Italian clothes were better.[60] She said:

> I remember my first day at school was terrible. Dressed with my Italian clothes . . . they were better than theirs, but I was a different style. So you know, they laugh at you. So I used to cry. And the kids would . . . I didn't understand what they were saying, but I could see that they were laughing at me. Now God knows what they were saying to me.[61]

Both male and female immigrants were taunted into dressing in American fashions. However, female immigrants also had to deal with American notions of beauty, which were often at odds with their ethnic standards. Some students also endured having their looks scrutinized by school counselors, who would write subjective and inappropriate comments about them.

One major difference between American standards of beauty and those of ethnic cultures involved weight. American women strive to be thin. Other cultures find plump women more attractive. The comment, "What a handsome woman, such a fine double chin!" was flattering to a woman in late-nineteenth-century, early-twentieth-century Jewish society.[62] One Jewish woman, Katya Govsky, described her mother as both "a beautiful woman" and "a very heavy fat woman." The descriptions were not contradictory to her.[63]

This was not the case for some Jewish Americans in 1950. There were two students who had accepted the idea that they had to be thin in order to be attractive. One Jewish American girl was having problems at school because she was overweight.[64] She said that the other students would laugh at her and deprecate her because of her appearance.[65] She also said that she could not concentrate on her schoolwork because she became too self-conscious about her appearance.[66] When a school counselor asked a Jewish American girl what kind of person she would like to be, she strove to be "thinner, taller, have longer hair, be prettier. . . ." In other words, she wanted to be attractive by American standards instead of Jewish ones, that is, fat, double chin, and wide hips.[67]

Moreover, school counselors made judgments about the attractiveness of Jewish American girls in their reports. Their judgments were based on American standards of beauty rather than in terms of what was considered attractive within Jewish culture. In the 1950s, one counselor wrote that his client "would be very good looking if she weighed twenty-five pounds less."[68] In another report, a female counselor described a student in the following manner:

> Her hips are wide and her bosom contours are like those of a fat man. Her clothing, consisting of a red corduroy jumper and pink, well-washed sweater did nothing to make her attractive.[69]

This was the same student who was mentioned previously as having problems at school because she was overweight. Other students were degrading her because of her weight and the counselor, whom she turned to for help, was doing the exact same thing to her on paper. The next time the girl visited the counselor, it was written that "her dress accentuates how fat she is."[70]

It is now understood by cultural historians and medical doctors that notions of attractiveness are subjective. The lack of conformity is best shown in the following student's session with a female counselor.

> Her hands are very small and fat, with fingers so short and pudgy they look deformed. The nail on the middle finger of her right hand was bitten to the quick but other nails were nicely filed.[71]

In another session, R. held up her hands and said that they were the ugliest hands that she had ever seen.[72] The male counselor wrote, "I pointed out to her that she had lovely tapering fingers and that her nails were well-manicured."[73] It was possible that R.'s middle nail had grown since the first session, but it is not possible for her hands to change so drastically from being pudgy and deformed to lovely and tapering between sessions. Both counselors were stating their own personal opinions about what they thought was attractive.

Moreover, there are doctors who think that these descriptions are inappropriate. On June 24, 2000, Ronald Sams, a medical doctor at Sibley Medical Center in Dolton, Illinois, explained during an interview that when describing a patient's appearance general comments are written.[74] He said:

> The patient's appearance is described in terms such as "well nourished," "no acute distress." You do not include whether or not you found them attractive. You comment on poor hygiene. You write whether or not the patient is alert.[75]

However, mental health specialists such as Kevin Robinson, a fellow in child psychology and sociology at St. Vincent Hospital in New York, persist in their belief that notions of attractiveness are universal and that the school counselors did not act inappropriately. They were simply following the norms of their profession. He said:

> In the appearance section [of the report], you just comment on your first impression of the patient before they talk. Note how tall a patient is, their attractiveness or unattractiveness, do they walk funny, whether or not they are well groomed or disheveled. . . . You can make subjective comments and write anything you want.[76]

However, he admitted that the counselors "took certain liber-ties" when writing their observations.[77] He said that "comments on weight are appropriate, but to say that the patient could stand to lose twenty-five pounds is not appropriate."[78]

Perhaps it is wrong to judge the practices and beliefs of one profes-sion against another. Possibly the school counselors were merely acting in accordance with the procedures of their profession. But the mental health profession's notion that attractiveness is universal across cultures is mistaken. Notions of attractiveness were not even the same between two counselors working at the same school. Fur-thermore, the practice of disregarding cultural notions of attractive-ness and choosing to use American standards or personal standards of beauty was harmful to immigrant girls. They sought help from counselors because students were teasing them about their appear-ance, but their efforts were in vain. The school counselors held the same beliefs as the students who teased them and offered no advice to remedy the situation.

Moreover, there was evidence that some immigrant girls were aware that the school counselors were judging them. In each ses-sion, one counselor noted whether the student wore a headscarf, or a babushka.[79] The student probably saw the therapist staring at her and felt she had to justify her appearance. The first time she said that she was babysitting and that her hair was in pin curls for a party later.[80] The next time she said that the children she babysat were unruly and she did not get a chance to straighten up before coming.[81] Incidentally, the first time the counselor wrote that the girl wore a headscarf. Wearing a scarf to set hair for a party later was a socially acceptable habit of American women. The second time the counse-lor wrote that the girl was wearing a babushka. Wearing a scarf to hide a lack of grooming was not a socially accepted American habit; the girl was acting like an immigrant.

A more profound example involved a Jewish girl who overdosed on barbiturates in 1957. A counselor at Austin High School in Chi-cago wrote that the girl "attributed her attempt at suicide to be the doctor's critical attitude toward her."[82] This near-death incident bears testimony to the fact that the girl was aware that she was being scrutinized. She also understood the outcomes of assimila-tion. A counselor wrote that "she felt that if she doesn't dress and act differently from her peers, she will lose her identity."[83] Assimilation was a drastic all-or-nothing process. Immigrants' cultural norms were looked down upon, while American habits were presented as desirable. Because she was not encouraged to choose which American habits to incorporate and which of her ethnic habits to retain, she thought that acting and dressing like an American meant that she had to stop acting and looking like herself.[84]

Immigrant Students Were Excluded

The last objective of civic education was to provide open opportunities for rational participation in group life in increasingly larger units, but Americanization did not always lead to integration. Immigrants lived in their own separate ethnic communities. When the High School Movement caused schools to become ethnically diverse, parents from the community protested to keep ethnic groups separate. In schools that were already diverse, immigrant students experienced social isolation because of nativist attitudes. Moreover, the push for civic education increased nativist feelings among American-born students. Nativist practices were aimed at immigrant children and teachers.

During the early part of the twentieth century, Chicago was composed of segregated ethnic communities.[85] When immigrants migrated to Chicago, they moved into their respective ethnic communities. Religious and ethnic conflicts occurred among them, which was reflected in the schools. Conspiracy theories were spread by Protestants, Catholics, and Jews. Protestants claimed that Catholics were taking over the board of education and that they were trying to place Catholics in administrative and supervisory positions.[86] They also accused Catholics of conspiring to gain control over school records by offering secretarial training.[87]

Catholics in turn accused Protestants of preventing them from holding important administrative positions. They maintained that the Chicago Principals' Club was dominated by Masons who blocked the appointment of Catholic principals.[88] They also claimed that the Ku Klux Klan had a representative present at all the meetings of the board of education.[89] Finally, Christians contended that

Jewish holidays disrupted the schools and that there were too many Jewish high school teachers.[90]

Politicians such as Thompson capitalized on ethnic animosities among male voters to get elected.[91] Many female immigrants were not involved in politics because they lacked U.S. citizenship.[92] Thompson's tactics included distributing pro-German handbills with pictures of his opponent that were anti-German in Czech and Polish neighborhoods in order to win the mayoral election in 1915.[93] In 1919, he won reelection by gathering support from German Chicagoans.[94] In 1927, he pushed textbooks that integrated Polish, German, French, and Irish stories into American history in order to gain support from those ethnic groups.

Although Thompson tried to integrate schoolbooks, the public schools in Chicago remained segregated. Children went to school and socialized with other children from their community. For example, Margaret Sabella, who lived in Bridgeport, a predominately Italian community in Chicago during the 1920s and 1930s, recalled that her social world was limited to Italians.[95]

> At the time I was a child everyone on our street, everyone—there was an exception, the Burns family was an Irish family—everyone was Italian. My little world consisted of three or four blocks. That wasn't a large area. I thought the whole world was Italian at that time. All my parents' friends who came over, they were all Italian.[96]

When ethnic groups such as Poles shared neighborhoods, social mixing did not occur. Emma Kowalenko wrote that, in 1910, "Language, parishes, Polish ethnic fraternal organizations, and small businesses owned by the same national group all kept this group segregated."[97]

Before Edwin Cooley became superintendent in 1900, patronage politics kept the public school teaching staff segregated.[98] Teachers were hired by local school committees of the board of education and were usually placed in the same neighborhoods in which they grew up.[99] Cooley ended this practice by submitting a list of all personnel appointments to the school management committee. If anyone tried to use political influence to affect the placement of a teacher, both parties would be exposed and the teacher would be placed on the ineligible list.[100]

During the 1929–1930 school year, the board decided to open Burbank Junior High School for seventh and eighth graders in an effort to alleviate overcrowding in several schools, which inadvertently caused Burbank Junior High School to become ethnically diverse. Several parents from the Lovett school district requested a conference with Mr. H. Wallace Caldwell, the president of the board of education, to protest. Mr. Caldwell reported:

> At a conference with me, a statement was made that parents south of the Chicago Milwaukee and St. Paul Railroad tracks do not want their children to attend schools with the Greeks, Italians, and Poles. I informed the committee that the public schools could not countenance such un-American doctrine, that it is the duty of the public schools to bring cooperation of all groups within the city.[101]

Although the board's official position was to integrate its schools and promote the High School Movement, it allowed parents to segregate their children. It issued permits allowing children to attend other schools. It also excused parents who kept their children out of school in protest by not enforcing the Compulsory Education laws. Rather than accusing these parents of being eugenicists, Caldwell implied that they were acting under the influence of someone else. He stated:

> The fact that only nine pupils from the Lovett district are out of school indicates these concessions have been acceptable to the overwhelming majority of the people of the district. In conclusion, I am decidedly of an opinion that some rebellion has been fermented by an outsider living many miles from the Burbank neighborhood. This person has opposed the junior high school from the start and constantly attempts to stir up trouble at the least opportunity, no matter what section of the city is involved. Further concessions seem to me to be unwarranted. If a small coterie of objections can persuade the school authorities to recede, the whole high school movement is jeopardized.[102]

The parents had no reason to continue their protest in light of the generous concessions made to them that allowed their children to attend school with children from ethnic groups that they deemed desirable.

Immigrant students who attended integrated schools experienced social isolation. Margaret Sabella learned this "from listening to those people who grew up on the West Side, Taylor Street. They said they were ostracized in school by other ethnic groups. They were looked down upon. They felt ashamed."[103]

Although Margaret Sabella was describing incidents from the beginning of the High School Movement in the 1920s and 1930s, students who were not members of the dominant ethnic group were still experiencing similar events in the 1950s. A counselor reported that a Jewish high school student with polio was being teased and feeling excluded.[104] The student described herself as "a little girl who was different, wasn't liked, and was not invited to parties."[105] In 1950, another student, a German American girl, thought that other students treated her with disinterest. [106] When she tried to initiate conversations, she felt that the other students gave her quick answers.[107] She said that they were not friendly or kind to her.[108] She also expressed that it was important for her to be involved in social activities with other students at school. Her counselor wrote:

> She commented that she shouldn't say it, but social things are making school better at this time. . . . D. thought it was little things like her class ring, membership in the Honor Society, and a party which the students are planning which are helping. Some parts of school are still unhappy but D. guesses she will stick it out.[109]

Her statements implied that feeling isolated and not being able to take part in the group life at school were factors in immigrant students' decisions to drop out of school. They would then be able to retreat back into the safety of their own ethnic neighborhoods.

A local newspaper in Chicago, the *Austin News*, published survey results indicating that civics education may have influenced students' beliefs about racial and ethnic segregation. In 1958, the impact of the social studies classes on students' citizenship beliefs was measured by the YMCA using a survey given to three hundred Austin High School students enrolled in social studies classes.[110] According to the results published in the *Austin News*, 22 percent of students polled felt that pupils of all races and nationalities should not attend school together everywhere in all states.[111] Because Chicago was composed of segregated ethnic communities and Jim Crow laws were in effect in the South and other areas of the United States during the 1950s, it was possible that the students believed that schools should be segregated before they enrolled in social studies classes. Since the newspaper did not publish information regarding students' beliefs about segregation prior to enrolling in social studies classes, there was no way of knowing the extent to which social studies classes influenced their beliefs. The published results of the survey were only useful in providing evidence that such a belief existed and was shared by sixty-six out of the three hundred high school students surveyed in 1958.

Nativist practices also occurred within the schools. They were aimed at teachers as well as students. For example, in 1900, school trustees complained to the board of education that "teachers do not understand the language and can not use or teach it correctly."[112] District superintendents defended the teachers, claiming that the charges were exaggerated and that the teachers were speaking "Chicagoese."[113] Superintendent Sabin explained: When the teachers use bad English they simply lapse into the Chicago dialect in which they were brought up. They are nearly all Chicago born.[114] The majority of the teachers may have been Chicago born. Many of them were also the children of immigrants and graduates of Catholic secondary schools. (See Table 4.)

According to 1908 Immigration Commission reports, there were 6,160 Chicago public school teachers in the elementary grades.[115] Half of those teachers, 3,125, were native born of a foreign father.[116] However, 2,031 out of 3,985 teachers who taught for ten years or more were native born of a foreign-born father.[117] Therefore the majority of the teachers who were employed in 1900 when the school trustees complained to the board were the children of immigrants. Complaining that the teachers could not speak English and therefore were not qualified to teach it was nativist and possibly anti-Catholic. By 1902, 66 percent of the candidates who passed the Chicago Normal School exam were graduates of Catholic secondary schools.[118]

One example of a nativist practice aimed at students occurred on December 3, 1919. Parker High School held a contest called Parsnips, Pumpkins, and Patriotism. The rules and regulations were that entrants must be American born; must be descendents of Miles

TABLE 4: Number of Elementary School Teachers, 1908

Ethnicity	No. of Years							Total
	<5	5–9	10–14	15–20	20–24	25–29	30<	
Native-born of native father								
White	282	518	585	446	333	227	101	2,492
black	3	5	3	2	2	0	0	15
Native-born of foreign father								
Bohemian	11	10	11	5	1	1	0	39
Canadian	24	30	35	27	15	9	2	142
Canadian French	1	3	0	3	1	3	0	11
Danish	5	10	6	4	0	0	0	25
Dutch	3	6	3	3	7	1	0	23
English	32	44	61	60	43	24	14	278
French	8	7	5	3	6	1	4	34
German	58	115	144	118	70	29	18	552
Jew, German	12	20	19	16	5	3	0	75
Jew, Polish	1	3	3	0	0	0	0	7
Jew, Russian	1	3	1	0	0	0	0	5
Jew, Other	12	6	3	1	2	2	0	26
Irish	175	336	345	285	154	87	45	1,427
Italian, North	0	0	0	1	0	80	0	1
Magyar	0	1	0	2	0	0	0	3
Norwegian	6	21	22	13	13	0	1	83
Polish	1	1	0	0	0	0	0	2
Russian	0	0	0	3	0	0	0	3
Scotch	14	28	29	27	30	19	5	152
Scotch-Irish	2	4	16	10	21	7	3	63
Slovak	3	0	0	0	0	0	0	3
Spanish	0	2	1	0	0	0	0	3
Swedish	27	36	28	12	6	7	1	117
Welsh	3	9	14	4	6	11	4	51
Total (native-born) 5,632								

Standish, Pocahontas, John Alden, George Washington, Patrick Henry, or George Cohan; and canned goods must be made of American tin, sealed in American solder, or must be in American jars and sealed with American wax.[119]

The first rule, "Entrant must be American born," excluded immigrant students from the contest. The second rule barred U.S.-born children of immigrants (with the exception of the Irish), especially those who did not have relatives on board the *Mayflower*. The last rule required that no foreign element be present in the canning process. The criteria privileged English-speaking Northern Europeans

TABLE 4: Number of Elementary School Teachers, 1908 *(continued)*

Ethnicity	<5	5–9	10–14	15–20	20–24	25–29	30<	Total
Foreign-born								
Bohemian	0	0	1	0	0	0	1	2
Canadian	4	16	13	11	11	3	0	58
Danish	2	2	6	0	2	0	0	12
Dutch	2	2	0	1	0	0	0	5
English	10	11	15	14	11	7	5	73
Flemish	0	0	1	0	1	0	0	2
French	1	3	4	0	0	0	1	9
German	8	10	30	21	20	7	2	98
Jew, German	3	2	4	2	1	1	0	13
Jew, Polish	0	7	2	0	0	0	0	9
Jew, Russian	2	5	2	0	0	0	0	9
Jew, Other	2	9	0	0	0	0	0	11
Irish	11	21	20	4	19	13	4	92
Italian, North	0	0	1	0	0	0	0	1
Italian, South	0	1	0	0	0	0	0	1
Magyar	1	1	0	0	0	0	0	2
Norwegian	0	5	5	5	3	0	0	18
Polish	0	1	0	0	0	0	2	3
Russian	1	0	0	0	0	0	0	1
Scotch	6	9	16	9	12	8	4	64
Scotch-Irish	0	4	0	0	0	3	0	7
Slovenian	0	2	0	0	0	0	0	2
Swedish	5	13	9	2	2	1	0	32
Welsh	0	1	1	1	0	0	1	4
Total (foreign-born) 528								
Total (both) 6,160								

Source: 61st Congress, 3rd Session, Reports of the Immigration Commission, *The Children of Immigrants in Schools*, vol. 2 (New Brunswick, NJ: Scarecrow Reprint Corporation, 1970), 681–682.

over non-English-speaking Southern and Eastern Europeans and asserted the dominance of Anglo Americans in defining what it means to be an American.

Sometimes nativist practices, such as political witch hunts, were aimed at both teachers and students simultaneously. For example, on November 16, 1919, high school and grade school principals rallied to "drive the Reds out of schools."[120] They were concerned that certain students and teachers were spreading bolshevism in the schools and they planned to expel the students and fire the teachers.[121]

In the 1930s, the board of education was paranoid over the spread of communism in Chicago's public schools. The board worked in conjunction with the American Legion and the Illinois Society of Colonial Dames, among others, to stamp out what they defined as "anti-American elements."[122] Tactics such as community patrols and oaths of allegiance were used to combat the perceived "communist scare."

In 1932, community patrol groups such as the Albany Park Women's Club were on alert for young communist activities in the schools.[123] On May 9, 1934, the following resolution, which requested the Illinois legislature to enact a law for all public employees to take an oath of allegiance, was adopted by the board:

> Be it resolved by the board of Education of the City of Chicago that it hereby endorses and requests immediate passage by the legislature of the state of Illinois of a law making it mandatory on all public employees of this state, including all public school teachers, principals and other employees of the boards of Education of the state annually to take and subscribe to the following oath, to-wit: "I solemnly swear to support the Constitution of the United States of America and the Constitution of the State of Illinois and the laws of the United States and the State of Illinois reverence for law and order, and undivided allegiance to the Government of the United States." And be it further resolved, that failure to take and subscribe to such oath shall make it unlawful for the person refusing to take such oath to hold public office or be employed by any and all governmental bodies within the State of Illinois.[124]

The oath was in compliance with a resolution introduced in the U.S. Congress on May 8, 1934, by Representative Edward Kenney, demanding that all public school teachers swear an oath to uphold the federal constitution.[125]

Even though teachers sometimes shared similar plights with students, it did not mean that they formed a kinship with immigrant students. Dominic Pandolfi, a child of Italian immigrants, recalled an incident involving his third-grade teacher circa 1916. He said:

> The school was rather tough. The teachers were very strict. They used to be difficult once in a while. But, we never forgot we were Italians and foreigners. I remember one [incident] . . . when I was in the third grade, the teacher had given us . . . we have a painting lesson, an art

lesson. Just to give you an indication of what could happen at that time. I was very poor in drawing. I remember it was a tulip I tried to draw, and she was upset because I made such an awful painting.[126]

His teacher then became progressively more abusive toward him.

She took me by the arm and took me into the eighth grade classroom, where the principal was. . . . She said look at what he did in his art. I was made to stand before the whole class. She kept berating me and then I started to laugh just out of nervousness. [She said] "Oh you think it's funny." She took me out into the hall and we had a red rubber hose, a thick one, 3/4" and she folded it in two and whipped me across the leg.[127]

Her overreaction to the drawing indicated that she was waiting for her moment to assert her dominance over him. First she tried embarrassment by sending him to the principal and belittling him in front of the class. Dominic's laughter gave him the upper hand in that the teacher thought he was mocking her in front of the class. In the end, she was able to overpower him physically by beating him. However, Dominic had an advantage. Although they were immigrants, his parents were aware of their rights and tried to seek justice for him. He also mentioned his parents' literacy, implying that he saw it as power.

My mother was very aggressive and she was one of the few who could read and write and my father also. . . . She marched over to a factory where one of the superintendents was a member of the school board. He saw what happened. So he went back [to the teacher] and I was scolded about it. The teacher never let me forget it. [She said] "This is the one that's so smart. He went to a member of the board of education." Things weren't so pleasant for a while for me because of that.[128]

The teacher's act of retaliation underscored the fact that she wanted to dominate him. The idea that someone of authority such as a member of the board of education would take his side incensed her more. Again, Dominic gained the upper hand. Hence her comment, "This is the one that's so smart." In her eyes, he was an enemy that she had to defeat and not a third grader who needed help drawing a tulip.

After examining the stated objectives of civics training and the actual practices and outcomes, I came to the conclusion that the Chicago Board of Education's success in Americanizing immigrant students from ethnic minority groups was not solely contingent on teaching immigrant students to think, act, and look like Americans. It was equally important for members of the board, American-born students, and teachers to recognize that assimilated immigrants and the children of immigrants were now Americans and to include them in the group life of the school. Accounts from immigrant students, statements from the board, and quotes from ethnic newspapers indicated that immigrant students from ethnic minority groups were still perceived as foreigners after assimilation.

Investigative reports, board reports, counselors' reports, accounts from immigrants, and a citizenship belief survey showed that the failure to incorporate the experiences of ethnic minority groups in civic education courses, the general disregard for ethnic culture in various aspects of school life, and nativist attitudes and practices resulted in feelings of isolation among immigrant ethnic groups and the exclusion of ethnic minority students by students from the dominant group.

Because civics education excluded the history of the local communities where the immigrant students lived and the history of their native lands as it related to their experiences in America, immigrants and children of immigrants were not able to see their lives as part of the American past. Immigrant students were expected to disregard the history of their parents' homelands without giving them new origins in America to build upon. Although some students were American born, the history of their parents' homeland included them as descendants. Moreover, the failure to relate the experiences of immigrants to American history taught native-born students that they were foreigners and not new Americans.

The push for Americanism to ensure political loyalty was important for the stability of the government and American society, but the methods used in achieving this goal also caused American-born people to view immigrants as possessing ideas that were different and opposed to their own. For example, the political witch hunts within the schools made teachers and students from different ethnic groups dangerous enemies. Derogatory statements from board of education officials implying that the foreign-born population was composed of anarchists and presidential assassins did nothing to alleviate these feelings.

Americanization programs that taught American habits to children failed to realize that immigrant children do not live at school. The board of education underestimated the influence of parents on their children's lives and previous cultural experiences. Children were not blank slates. Instead of expanding immigrant students' previous identity and notions of self to include being American, Americanization programs tried to eradicate their language and ethnic cultural habits.

There was no reciprocity. American students learned nothing about the habits of immigrant students. The curriculum privileged American habits, making them the standard. This is not to imply that American students should be taught to act like foreign people, but they should at least understand that immigrant students are different.

Being teased about their clothing and appearance made immigrant students feel inferior. Some students accepted the notion that looking like an American was better than looking like themselves and other members of their ethnic group. Immigrant girls were especially vulnerable to self-esteem issues. They had to conform to American notions of beauty, which were in opposition to their own cultural norms of attractiveness.

Americanized students were different from the people in their native homelands and sometimes their own parents in language, history, dress, and culture. Yet they were not considered Americans. Ethnic animosities against them persisted. Students from the dominant American culture did not socialize with them. Xenophobia possibly created by the social studies curriculum caused other students to see them as distinct people, not American. Nativist practices within schools reinforced these notions. They were outsiders in two cultures because the Chicago Board of Education used the public schools to change immigrant students without changing the way American students viewed immigrant and ethnic minorities.

CHAPTER 4

Old World Influences on Attitudes toward Schooling in the New World

Jewish, Southern Italian, Polish, and Irish Catholic immigrant women brought several important attitudes toward schooling from their homelands to America. The fundamental belief that formal education was more important for male children than female children was present both in the Old World and among immigrants in the New World. Another belief was that girls would be better prepared for their future roles as wives and mothers by fulfilling familial obligations and serving as helpmates to their mothers instead of attending school. These attitudes were intergenerational and shared across immigrant cultures. Although class, politics, and ethnic discrimination shaped immigrants' educational experiences, gender was a major determinant in the length and type of schooling children received and in parental attitudes toward formal education.

Jewish Attitudes and Schooling Experiences in Eastern Europe

Historians such as Leonard Dinnerstein generally argue that Jewish immigrant culture stressed the importance of education, often citing the adage, "The Jew without learning is incomplete. A little better than an animal."[1] It meant that education was fundamental to the development of a person. However, parental attitudes toward formal education and the schooling experiences of immigrant students often differed according to gender. After primary lessons in reading and writing, Jewish children received the education deemed appropriate for their future roles in life. Formal education was stressed for male children to prepare them for the life of respect and prestige as a scholar or rabbi. Informal education was given to female children to prepare them for their roles as wife and mother.

In the East European *shtetl* or village, Jewish boys were encouraged to become talmudic scholars, the men who both studied and interpreted the holy books and the laws of God. Talmudic scholars were highly regarded. People thought they were wise, sought their advice, and respected their judgment. It was also assumed that they would be ideal husbands and good fathers.[2] The role of talmudic scholar required an extensive amount of formal education. In the early twentieth century, it was restricted to males.

In the home, mothers encouraged their sons to become scholars. At an early age, they recited this nursery rhyme to their male babies, which reflected their hopes for the future: "Sleep soundly at night and learn Torah by day. And thou'lt be a Rabbi when I have grown grey."[3] Throughout childhood, male children were taught to revere books, to remain quiet while their father studied, and to treat learned guests with respect.[4] After the age of four, boys began their formal education and were treated with the respect due to a student.[5]

This was not the case for girls. Jewish girls, such as Fannie Shapiro, in late-nineteenth-century–White Russia, were allowed to receive some schooling but not as much as their brothers.[6] Fannie recalled:

> After a while, my mother thought I had enough, I didn't need any more education. That was getting me angry and that was when I started planning quietly to come to America for an education. My father thought I didn't have enough, but my mother. . . . But the boys, they never had enough. My two brothers went into the village to *cheder* (elementary school for boys). They had to take up a higher education, the kind that's not for girls—*Gemara* (a religious school). . . . When my brothers went to school, I was at home helping my mother. . . . There were other children. We were six of us so I had to help her. I had to wash laundry. I had to help her with a lot of things and she used to watch that I don't do anything wrong with *flayshig* (meat/poultry) and *milchik* (dairy products).[7]

A few Jewish girls, mostly from upper-class families, had more educational opportunities and more career choices. For example, Kataya Govsky, who lived in Russia from 1906 to 1923, had a mother who was a university professor and a father who was a laborer. [8] There was somewhat of a role reversal in which her mother, a female, was the scholar in the home and her sister was educated for a profession while her father worked. She said: My sister, the doctor, she's like Mama, brilliant. My mother used to read night and day. She didn't know anything about housework.[9]

She also mentioned that girls were allowed to attend secular private schools if their parents could afford to send them. She said:

And we children (Kataya and her sister) could afford to go to pretty expensive private schools—*gymnaziia* they call it. There were Jewish schools because the Russian schools allowed in only 5 percent of Jews. But the children of the better class of Russian Jews who lived in cities were all educated.[10]

Because 5 percent of Jews were allowed to attend Russian public schools and only the elite could afford to pay for private school, the majority of Jews had no formal education.

Anuta Sharrow, another Jewish immigrant from Russia, had a similar experience. She said:

My father was anxious to give me education: music education and general education. My parents themselves weren't educated except in Jewish [Yiddish language and Jewish culture]. So they felt that it would be a pride for their children to be, you see. That's one thing. The other thing, he was able to support me. He had financial means to send me to school. I remember when I was a teenager, even younger, I said to my father, "I don't want any dresses, no clothing, nothing. Just send me to high school." They call it *gymnaziia* in Kiev. . . . At that time, the Jews couldn't teach, they couldn't enter schools, unless they were rich maybe. You had to pay for everything. That's why my father paid for me.[11]

Anuta Sharrow also acknowledged that her experiences were not typical of all Jewish women. She made this observation:

There, in the little towns, Jewish women were limited. There were no schools; so they were far away from the language, and from the

Russian culture. Only those that went to school in a big city like Kiev had a chance. In the towns, they were locked up at home with housework.[12]

In addition to gender role expectations and class, politics also affected the education of Jewish girls. Tsilia Michlin Goldin from Bobruisk, Byelorussia, could not finish school for political reasons because her family was forced to live underground during World War I. After the war ended, she still could not attend school because of her gender. She had to assume the responsibility of the household and take care of her younger siblings because her mother was sick. By the time her mother recovered circa 1925, she encountered more political opposition. The Russian government closed all the Jewish schools. Jews were denied access to the public schools unless they denounced their religion.[13] This also created class issues since she was denied a formal education because her father could not afford a tutor. She said:

> I wanted an education, but because I hadn't finished primary school, I couldn't continue. Because my father was a religious man and a Jew, his children were denied access to the public school. The authorities knew that my father wouldn't stop his religious practices. And of course the Jewish schools had been closed. My dream had been to get an education and become proficient in something so that I could teach, or I would have liked to become a tailor, to work with clothing. I couldn't get into professional school, and my father could not afford to bring in someone who would give me private tutoring. So it was impossible for me to receive a formal education.[14]

Julia Zissman Umanstev, a middle-class Jew, was also denied schooling for political reasons. She fled Moscow with her mother during the World War II Nazi invasion. By wearing a disguise, she was able to go to school in Tashkent.[15] She stated:

> I was able to go to school because we lived with a very intellectual Uzbek family, very rich. The man, who was a Muslim, had four wives. . . . The children went to Russian schools, learned Russian, French, English. They taught music too. I attended the same grade as one of the man's oldest daughters, who was my friend. . . . had to wear a *chadra*, the traditional Islamic dress for women. I, a Jewish girl, had to wear a Muslim outfit! I had forty-two braids, the whole thing. You had to look like one of them, or you could be killed![16]

As an adult, Julia was able to finish medical school in 1954 because her husband and her mother assumed the child-rearing responsibilities. She said:

Alex was born in 1952, while I was still at school. My husband took care of him most of the time. He was writing his dissertation, so he could stay at home to study and take care of Alex. My mother helped on the weekends.[17]

Anya Pavel, whose mother was a doctor and whose father was a construction engineer and chief of a large building company, was also able to attend school in Bobruisk, Russia, during the late 1950s and 1960s. However, anti-Semitism limited the type of education she could receive. She recalled:

When I was in the ninth grade, in the last months of my mother's life, I spoke to her in the hospital of my dream of becoming a doctor. And my mother told me, "You can't do it because it is impossible now for a Jew in Russia to enter medical school. You shouldn't dream about it. You should go to technical college."[18]

She was able to enter technical college as opposed to medical college or even law school because no oral exam was required for admission.[19] The written exam was anonymous, so no one knew that she was Jewish.[20]

According to the accounts of Russian Jews, education for Jewish children in the Old World was differentiated according to gender-specific roles determined by Jewish culture, especially among the lower-middle classes. The amount of schooling, which was also a factor in the type of occupation a male student would have in the future, was based on the family's ability and desire to pay. Among the middle- to upper-class elite, some girls experienced more gender equity in schooling and in occupational choice than their poorer counterparts. Elite women like Kataya Govsky's mother, Julia Umanstev, were freed of traditional gender role expectations, such as household chores and child rearing that limited education for the majority of Jewish girls. Even they were exceptional since only 5 percent of the total literate population graduated from a secondary school in 1897.[21] Moreover, government-sanctioned anti-Semitism during World War I and II as well as anti-Semitic attitudes in the 1950s and 1960s hindered education for all Russian Jews, male and female, regardless of class.

Literacy was also limited for the majority of the Jewish population in Poland. There were public elementary schools in Russian-dominated Poland in 1906, but anti-Semitism prevented Jewish children from attending. Although there were no laws restricting the number of Jews attending public school, the schools practiced anti-Semitism. Jewish parents complained that their children's applications were refused.[22] Moreover, Jewish children who were accepted were prevented from becoming literate because schools taught reading and writing on Saturdays.[23] Thus Jewish children were put at a disadvantage because they could not attend school on Saturday in observance of the Sabbath.

Only 17 percent of Jewish girls attended public elementary school in 1906.[24] Eighty percent of the Jewish population in Poland could not send their children to secondary school in 1906.[25] In addition, historians Neil M. Cowan and Ruth Schwartz Cowan reported that compulsory attendance was not universal and that most of the Jews who emigrated as adults after 1887 were not highly educated.[26] Women were at a greater disadvantage. They wrote: The men could read and write, at least in Yiddish . . . and perform rudimentary calculations. Many of the women, perhaps, a majority, were completely illiterate.[27]

They attributed this situation to school quotas (limiting the number of Jewish children allowed to attend school) that the Russian government sanctioned in Poland.[28]

*Cheder*s for girls were available by the turn of the twentieth century but only in the most progressive towns.[29] Jewish girls with "radical" or "assimilated" parents were allowed to attend.[30] An average of 5.8 percent of Jewish girls attended *cheder*, while 50 percent of boys attended *cheder*.[31]

Historians agree that most girls were taught basic literacy in Yiddish at home, but I could not locate any official records to back this claim.[32] Moreover, Beatrice C. Baskerville in her 1906 study of Polish Jews reported that in *cheder*, illiteracy was the norm because boys were not given appropriate learning materials or a qualified teacher. She wrote:

[The students] have no books, and could not read them if they had. The course is supposed to consist of instruction in writing and reading in Hebrew. The writing is generally left out of the program, and the reading is mostly done by the *melameds* [instructors] themselves. Some of them try to teach their pupils the rudiments of Russian grammar. I say "try," because the master knows so little about his subject that his lesson recalls the parable of the blind leading the blind.[33]

After compulsory education laws were passed in certain areas of Poland, Jewish girls and boys were expected to attend school. The government used schools to assimilate Jews. For example, Rose Sorkin, a Polish Jew who grew up during World War I in Semiatycze, Grodnogybernia (which was originally a part of Poland and later became a part of Russia), was forced to attend a public school, which was Catholic in denomination.[34] She remembered:

We all spoke Polish and we were all going to school. We had two schools, a Polish school and a folkschule (school for secular Jewish culture and Yiddish), and we had a Hebrew school for boys. You could attend all three, but you had to go to the Polish school. It was a must.[35]

The folkschule and the Hebrew school were necessary because the public schools stripped Jewish children of their culture by subjecting them to religious practices that were often in opposition to their own religion. Rose also described her experiences as a Jewish person who was forced to imitate the Catholics at her school:

In the Polish school, we had to stand on our knees on Sunday and sing, and we had to cross ourselves even if we were Jewish girls. Otherwise, they wouldn't let us go to the school. We couldn't get an education unless they wanted us to.[36]

Rose's experiences illustrate that assimilation is not a simple process for children. Based on Rose's choice of the words "forced" and "pushed," which describe acts of violence, she was a reluctant participant in the assimilation process.

Moreover, her country was in the midst of a world war and was twice invaded, first by the Russians and then by the Germans. She was of school age when she immigrated to the United States. Rose said:

Bolsheviks took over Poland. Then the Russians came in. They brought in Russian teachers, and we had to learn the Russian language and they made us sing in Russian, the Internationale in school. We had to talk Russian in the street when we got out from school. We had about three synagogues, but they burned them down. They didn't like the Jewish religion to be kept up. They wanted everybody to go with them, to be Russian. They didn't allow religion in school even. When the Germans came, we were forced to learn German. We were learning all kinds of German songs. We were young kids. Young kids are easier to learn, and to forget, than grown-ups. Everything was just come and go, you see. Here in the United States, we're doing things the American way. There we had to do the Polish way, we had to do Russian style, we had to do German style and we were pushed from one school to the other, and from one style to the other. Our education was very hard.[37]

Rose's account exemplifies an extreme form of cultural imperialism. The schools she attended were operating on several assumptions: that a child can forget his or her native culture easier than an adult can; that schools have unlimited influence on their students; and that assimilation is easy for children.

The first assumption was that because Rose was a child she could "forget" her native culture easier than an adult could. This was assumed even though she was a young child still living at home with her parents whose culture would inevitably influence her and would be reinforced in the home. Moreover, when she was still living in her native land, her ethnic community also reinforced her culture. Although Rose eventually immigrated to America, it was not uncommon for immigrants to huddle in various parts of town and establish Hebrew day schools, thereby preserving some elements of their culture.[38]

Jewish Attitudes and Schooling Experiences in the United States

Jewish immigrants also brought these notions of education—formal education for males and informal education for females—with them to America. In 1909, a journalist wrote, "The chief ambition of the new Jewish family in America is to educate our sons."[39] At about the same time, an immigrant New Yorker, who was a mother of five, wrote in a Yiddish newspaper that she refused to withdraw her fifteen-year-old son from school to work for her business because "he has inclinations to study and goes to school dancing. I lay great hopes on my child."[40]

However, the financial sacrifices made by immigrant families were not just for the success of their individual children. By educating their children, some Jewish parents were investing in their communities. One immigrant father underwent personal hardship to send his son to school so that he could have a better life and would be able to improve the lives of people within the Jewish community. He declared:

> It is enough that I am a merchant. . . . What is such a life? What can I do for my people or myself? My boy shall be a lawyer; learned and re-spected of men. And it is for that I stand here, sometimes when my feet ache so that I would gladly go and rest. My boy shall have knowl-edge. He shall go to college.[41]

Both parents wanted their male children to go into American professions that would earn them as much respect and prestige as a talmudic scholar would receive in Europe. Their sons would be-come doctors, lawyers, accountants, pharmacists, or teachers.[42] In this way, they would bring honor to themselves, their families, and communities.

Jews in other cities also shared this ambition. Surveys of students in Gary, Indiana, taken in 1917 revealed that hunger and sickness, such as amnesia from infected tonsils, adenoid problems, and dis-eased teeth, were the main reasons why children remained home or performed poorly in the classroom. They also found that immigrant parents regularly made financial sacrifices to keep their children in school.[43]

There was also a study on truancy and nonattendance in the Chi-cago public schools conducted by two social workers, Edith Abbott and Sophonisba P. Breckinridge during the early part of the twenti-eth century. They found that parents generally complied with com-pulsory attendance laws. Factors that contributed to noncompliance included poor health, inadequate clothing, chores, work, family fes-tivities such as weddings or funerals, religious holidays, and ignor-ance that school was free and attendance was mandatory.[44]

Moreover, before strict Illinois child labor laws were enacted and enforced in 1917, poverty was a legitimate excuse for noncompliance in Chicago. Under the old 1911 law, parents were able to plead poverty and put their children to work without evidence of age and with no education requirement except the ability to read and write a simple sentence, not necessarily in English.[45] Some poor parents still sent their children to school because of the changing nature of the economy that made the long-term benefits of staying in school outweigh the short-term gains. They were also offered financial assistance.

Abbott and Breckinridge discovered that because of changes in the structure of journeyman trade unions and the nature of the job market, children were no longer able to leave school to learn a trade.[46] On-the-job apprenticeships, which were usually offered to children, were rapidly becoming obsolete. Skilled labor positions now required certification, which was acquired by undergoing a certain amount of formal education. Because of the rise in industrial jobs, there was an increased demand for unskilled labor. As a result of their lack of certification, children usually ended up in entry-level factory jobs with almost no chance of promotion. Therefore social reformers in Chicago such as George Mead urged parents to forgo their children's menial financial contribution and keep them in school.[47] Ideally, schools would prepare children for better-paying professions with more job security, which would be essential for survival in their adult lives. As a result of Abbott and Breckinridge's findings, a conference was called in an attempt to change the child labor laws in 1913.[48]

Immigrant Jews in Chicago were also offered financial assistance in keeping their children in school from community service organizations such as the Scholarship and Guidance Association (SGA). The SGA formed from the work of two parallel agencies, the Joint Committee of Vocational Training for Girls and the Committee on Scholarship for Jewish Children. It originated in 1911 as the Joint Committee of Vocational Training of Girls, which formed for the purpose of securing employment for girls who dropped out of school at age fourteen. In 1912, it became coed and was called the Joint Committee for Vocational Supervision, later known as the Vocational Supervision League in 1913. After the passing of the first Illinois child labor law that required children to have a certification to enter industry, the Vocational Supervision League, working under the auspices of the Chicago Board of Education, secured employment that paid an average of ten to fifteen dollars a week for children between the ages of fourteen and sixteen or gave loans for them to continue in school.[49] In the 1930s, the Vocational Supervision League became the Children's Scholarship Association.

In 1915, the Chicago Women's Aid formed the Committee on Scholarships for Jewish Children, which was known as the Scholarship Association for Jewish Children from 1918 to 1942. In 1942, the Scholarship Association for Jewish Children became nonsectarian and interracial. It combined with the Children's Scholarship League and was thereafter known as the Children's Scholarship Association until 1945. In 1945, the Children's Scholarship Association changed its name to the Scholarship and Guidance Association (SGA) and expanded its services to offering guidance, the study of problems in parent-child relationships, assistance to guidance personnel of Chicago schools, and studies on dropouts.

According to its history, the SGA provided loans at first, then scholarships, which by 1916 were funded by the Chicago Board of Education.[50] An average of fifteen dollars a month was provided to supplement family income in order to meet the educational needs of children, including the purchase of clothing, lunches, books, and registration fees.[51]

Despite financial incentives and aid programs offered to both male and female Jewish students, all Jewish children were not encouraged to go to school and achieve academic success. For cultural reasons, formal education remained a male-oriented activity. Duties in the home prevailed over inclinations to achieve academic success. Fannie Shapiro discovered this when she immigrated to America in 1906. She stated:

> I was so naive and my whole hope [was] that I was coming to this country to get an education. I didn't realize. I didn't understand how things are. I heard so much about America: a free country for the Jews, and you can get an education, and you didn't have to pay for schooling. So I came. I didn't think. I didn't know. I never saw anybody working. I didn't know what it was all about. So I thought that I'll stay with family. I'll help probably in the house, with the children, wash the dishes, and I'll go school. But it didn't work out that way.[52]

Although Fannie had no children of her own, she was expected to assume most of the child rearing and household chores in her uncle's home while he and his wife worked in the family store.[53] Fannie discovered that things were not much different for her in America. The same expectations that she would be a helpmate rather than a scholar awaited her.

In 1924, Janet Sommers complained that her father wanted her to work instead of continuing her education. She said:

> I took a commercial course in high school, but he [her father] was annoyed with me. He was angry because he thought I should go out on my own and make a living. I was fourteen maybe closer to fifteen already. He was a dictator, a tyrant really.[54]

As late as 1950, an immigrant girl reported in an SGA counseling session that one night she had a substantial amount of homework to do and did it instead of washing the dishes.[55] Her mother "raised Cain." She felt that her daughter was neglecting her duties in the home. It was more important for her daughter to clean the house, which was both an immediate need and a duty that would prepare her for her role as a wife, than to devote her time to studies.

Sometimes duties in the home included work in the family business as well. In 1958, a Jewish girl, M., missed many days of school due to illness. Instead of sending her to summer school to make up the lost days, her parents sent her to work as an assistant with her father.[56] Again the immediate needs of the family took precedence over M.'s personal success in school.

Moreover, there is evidence that some Jewish girls did not share their parents' beliefs and were genuinely concerned about their formal education. M., for example, feared that "teachers would be mad at her if she didn't catch up on her work."[57] M. must have been an overachiever at some point because her report indicated that the school wanted to double promote her, but her mother intervened because achievement or success in school was taboo.[58] Another immigrant, Mollie Linker, who attended school in America in 1914, was also an overachiever, but was held back by her parents. She recalled the incident:

> When school was out in June, I knew I couldn't go back anymore, so coming home I cried all the way; and I was put in high fifth in less

than two months. . . . And I came home, it was on Friday, and I said to mother, "Ma, the teacher cried," and I broke out sobbing because I like school. My father had a job for me. I couldn't do anything.[59]

Mollie was only thirteen years old at the time. Although she did well in her classes and the child labor law in Illinois mandated that children attend school until the age of sixteen, Mollie was obligated by her father to work.

Another Jewish girl, who tried to educate herself, read too much for her mother's tastes. As a result, she was brought in for counseling for being, among other things, "withdrawn and living in books" as well as for "obesity and sloppiness."[60] Had this girl been born a boy exhibiting these traits (obesity and sloppiness aside), she would have been praised as being a model talmudic scholar.[61] The complaint against obesity also demonstrated a cultural adaptation. In the Old Country, Jewish women were to be praised for being heavy.[62]

Coincidentally, while Jewish girls were being sent to counseling by their mothers because of their overachievement, social workers and teachers were referring Jewish girls to counseling because of their underachievement.[63] This is a clear example of Jewish cultural values conflicting with the public schools. These Jewish girls were caught in the middle between what was expected of them by their parents and what their teachers and school officials expected of them.

Italian Attitudes and Schooling Experiences in Italy

Regional differences in parental attitudes toward education implicate class struggles in Italy. Historian Salvatore LaGumina argued that middle-class Northern Italians embraced public education, while poor Southern Italians shunned it, suspecting it of being a tool of the ruling class.[64]

In 1859, under a centralized schooling system in Italy, all Italians paid taxes to support public education, but all leadership positions were held by Northern Italians, who passed school mandates that benefited them and disadvantaged the Southern Italians. For example, the length of the school year was determined by the planting season. In Northern Italy, this season ended a month earlier than in the South.[65] However, all schools were scheduled to begin after the planting season ended in the North. Parents in Southern Italy, who were unable to plant their crops without the help of their children, sent their children to school a month after school started. This caused educational disparities between Northern Italian children and Southern Italian children.[66]

Moreover, inequalities in the distribution of wealth between Northern and Southern provinces aggravated educational disparities. Children who were able to attend school regularly and therefore able to advance beyond the primary level were middle class. Most of the students were middle class. Elena Teruty, an Italian immigrant from Naples, a Southern Italian province, who attended school in the 1930s, remarked:

> Mind you, most of the kids, they didn't go to school at home. If they went, it was just for a couple of years. I'm talking about middle class people. Some could not afford it. Even though the school was almost for free. A lot of people didn't have that kind of money. Most kids drop out. They go six years or ten years. That's the most. That's it. That was all the education you could get. Most people at that time in Italy were not educated.[67]

Poor Southern Italians also complained that the type of education offered in the schools was neither relevant nor adequate. In the late nineteenth, early twentieth century, an immigrant woman from Sant'Ilario stated: If our children don't go to school, no harm results. But if the sheep don't eat, they will die. The school can wait, but not our sheep. We say that the sheep must eat.[68]

In another account, an Italian woman summarized her brother's schooling experience between 1880 and 1920:[69]

> Well, he has gone to school. He learned to make a few scrawls on a piece of paper. He can read *zoppcando* (haltingly) out of a book. Now that this has been done, what good is it to him or any body else? He has not only wasted time but the family has had to go to the expense of buying blank books, primers, pen, pencil, and paper, and what has the family gotten out of all that? What use can we get out of going to school?[70]

Neither of these people viewed school as an investment. Sending their sons to school was perceived as a waste of time and money because schools did not address their immediate concerns, nor did they teach their students how to improve their families' way of life. In fact, the student described in the previous quote could barely read and write well enough to better his own station in life.

Parents also believed that the teachers reflected the traditions and values of the middle class because they were from the North.[71] They were concerned that their children would reject their family's way of life. A saying from the province of Basilicata reflected this sentiment: *Fesso chi fa i figli meglio di lui* (Stupid and contemptible is he who makes his children better than himself).[72]

There were also teachers who were biased against Southern Italian children. One Italian immigrant recalled the following from the early 1900s: When a boy was absent from school a few days, the teacher would question the boys and remark, "Well, his hand is better adapted to hold the *zappa* (hoe) than the pen."[73]

The boys who regularly attended school were seldom encouraged to do so by their teachers. They often heard teachers and school officials make remarks such as, "Of what use is school to you anyway? You'll always be a peasant."[74] These teachers wanted to maintain the social order—Southern Italians as peasant farmers on the bottom with little or no social mobility and Northern Italians at the top.

Those students who persisted in school despite the obstacles were physically and socially separated from their parents. Like Russian Jews who had to travel to Kiev to complete their education in the early part of the twentieth century, many Southern Italians living in rural communities had to travel to and reside in larger, urban communities, often in northern provinces, in order to continue their education beyond the primary grades.[75] Thus they were physically separated from their families.

While at school, children were able to socialize with people outside their families who did not necessarily share the values and beliefs of their parents.[76] This could lead to a weakening of familial ties and the child might begin to question familial values. Because students lived at school, more authority was given to teachers and school officials than the head of the family. As a result, students were socially separated from their families.

Moreover, the compulsory education law, which encompassed all students, male and female, clashed with parental values. The following accounts are about Southern Italian mothers who were concerned about their daughters' virtue and refused to let them go to school. One Italian immigrant woman said in the early 1900s:

> My mother explained to me the reason for her illiteracy. In her case, it was the fear of my grandparents that she would write love letters to young men in the town and this would trespass against the decorum of a well brought up Italian girl.[77]

Around 1896, another Italian American from Castelbuone, Sicily, recalled that one woman let her daughter attend school through the fourth grade. "And then because she grew up very fast and looked older than she really was, she had to leave school and stay at home and be a good young lady."[78]

Marietta Interlandi, an immigrant woman from Aacte, Italy, had an older sister who had a similar experience in the late 1890s, early 1900s.

> My sister went to the fifth grade, which they call it like eighth grade here. My sister was taken out of school a little of ahead of time, because she was so tall. Mother thought she didn't belong in school anymore. How do you like that? You see, when the girls grow up like that, it's just one of those things, they don't let them loose. You know, she was—she was a good-looking girl and she was tall and my mother says, "You stay home. You don't have to go to school."[79]

One girl was taken out of school because literacy would enable her to have illicit communication with men. The other girls were allowed to become somewhat literate, having reached the American equivalent of about an eighth grade education, but because they were physically mature, their mothers feared that they might commit sexual improprieties.

Moreover, poor Italians, like poor Jews, believed that the purpose of education for female students was to prepare them to work inside the home as a wife and mother. A girl's training was completed primarily at home by her own mother starting as early as four years old until she was considered an adult at about age eleven.[80] She was expected to help in the field, take care of smaller children, keep the house clean, attend the fire and water supply, and to learn a host of other domestic chores.[81]

Because school prolonged social infancy by delaying marriage, girls were often discouraged from going to school. Between 1880 and 1920, one mother stated:

> Three daughters of mine are well placed. My youngest is seventeen. With God's help, I hope she will not disappoint me by going to school. In that case, I may never be able to see my happy day when all my daughters are married and I don't have to worry any more.[82]

Italian Attitudes and Schooling Experiences in the United States

There was evidence that Southern Italian immigrants' attitudes and schooling experiences in the United States were affected by their experiences in Italy. There was opportunity to send their children to school, but regional differences as well as economic and gender issues persisted.

An Italian Chicagoan, Rosamond Mirabella, who was born to immigrant parents in 1886, described how the educational disadvantages in Southern Italy affected immigrants in the United States:

> [T]hey were mostly all illiterates. And their children all were made to go to school and all that because they felt and they realized how . . . what a time they had not being able to, you know. So they all believed . . . our people believed in learning. That's one thing I'll say about it. An Italian came to our house, was looking for Toto (her brother) and Toto at the time was up north. And he said to me . . . "Senora," he said, "I can't read nor write." He was speaking in Italian. He said, "but I swear to you that my son is going to have all the education possible." And years after that I met his son. And I don't remember whether he was a . . . in medicine or in law. Our people respect and like learning. That's one thing about our Italians.[83]

Regional differences between Northern and Southern Italians persisted in the United States. However, within the context of American society, racial or ethnic difference was more pronounced than class among Italian immigrants. Southern Italians immigrants were more likely to be subjected to stereotypes and were not able to assimilate as easily as their Northern counterparts. One Italian Chicagoan, Father Joachim Martorano, who was born in 1937, described this phenomenon in the 1980s:

> We were thought to have been the type of people who always carried a knife anyhow and looked to be very different as far as complexion was concerned. Especially I would say among the—the Italians with whom I associated, being more of the Sicilian Southern Italian type, rather than the Northern Germanic, blue-eyed blonde type Italian. So we were immediately noticeable and very different and when I can make that comparison now, like with black children, I can see how that was my experience as well and I feel a tremendous obligation to make that . . . make that point.[83]

Although some Southern Italian immigrant parents sent their children to school regularly, Northern Italian immigrant parents were more familiar with the rituals of schooling, such as instilling study habits, creating an environment for learning at home, and looking over completed homework assignments. As a result, their children were more easily assimilated and less likely to be singled out for racial differences at school than certain Southern Italian immigrant children. Such was the case with Mary Argenzio and Father Martorano.

Mary Argenzio, a child of Southern Italian immigrants, was born in Chicago in 1893. She recalled that her parents emphasized education but did not check her homework or ask her about it.[84] She knew that it was important because her father spoke of it as an investment and he sent her brother to the University of Illinois at Champaign-Urbana in 1898. She said:

> My father used to say that you can't lose an education, and that they . . . they had the money to send you. And my brother . . .72 years ago or more, he went to—I just said where he went—Champaign, yeah.[85]

Father Martorano spoke more about the familiarity that Northern Italian immigrants had with the rituals of going to school in the 1940s. He stated:

> It wasn't always just simply a question of German versus Italian, but there was a greater sense, I think, of studiousness on the part of the

Germanic kids, who would be rarely seen on the street after school.
They'd be at home doing their homework and studying as a matter of
course, whereas I'd get it in right before I went in the morning or you
know, that wasn't the kind of schooling that either my mom and dad
had or the rest of my family had . . . there wasn't a studious kind of at-
mosphere at home that would allow me to get in to studies. Where
some of the other kids, that was obvious that they came in with their
papers all crisp and clean and nothing was soiled, you know. And I
still can't spell, you know. And I'm not making an excuse, but there—
there's that kind of whole attitude and upbringing that had me more
on the streets than in my living room or kitchen table and that's
where we did any kind of studying.[86]

School and home were distinct entities for Father Martorano. He
was sent to school regularly, but his parents did not reinforce the
lessons learned at school. They also did not teach him "proper"
study habits.[87]

Moreover, the schools in the 1940s that Father Martorano attended had not recognized his needs in this regard. Instead, his academic failure was considered characteristic of the Italian "race." In
other words, the schools expected him to fail because he was Italian
and therefore racially different. He stated:

It was becoming more evident as I—as I progressed, you know, at St.
Michael's, to see that the differences became quite ethnic kinds of differences, rather than simply a question of intelligence or ability to
learn. And actually that is happening with other children now, you
know, but today the—the person who is Puerto Rican may be on the
lowest rung of the social ladder and pointed to as having a speech difference and obvious kind of physical difference, etc.[88]

Still, despite the racialization of Italian immigrants, there seemed
to be a more cooperative attitude among parents toward teachers in
America. The accounts of two children of immigrants, Lina Tarabori
and Mary Manella, confirm this. Lina Tarabori, an Italian Chicagoan
born in 1907, recalled how her parents supported her teacher's puni-
tive actions:

You had to do your homework and—you had to be good. And if you
came home and said the teacher spanked you, and I didn't do it, well,
maybe that's because another time she didn't see you and she didn't
spank you. So you got it now for then. So you decided you wouldn't

tell your mother when she give you a bawling out, because you didn't get any sympathy from her anyway. But whatever she did was the right thing to do and that's what the kids need today.[89]

Although she was born in Chicago almost twenty years later, Mary Manella witnessed the same degree of trust and cooperation among her parents and her teachers. She said:

[W]e were taught and we were brought up in a home where the school, the teachers, the officials, they were always right . . . no matter what. You did not come home and complain. And if you did, you were reprimanded at home in addition to being reprimanded at school. . . . And the teacher was always sort of held up as person to be respected . . . her authority. Her I say because we only had female teachers in grade school.[90]

In the early twentieth century, Italian immigrant narratives also indicate that there were conflicts over the compulsory school laws in the United States. Some immigrant parents tried to use some of the same cultural and economic reasons for keeping their children out of school as they did in Italy.

An Italian immigrant mother, who found it disgraceful that she had to work outside the home to supplement her husband's earnings, tried to skirt around the attendance laws. She explained:

In our old village [near Caltanisetta in Sicily] it was shameful for a wife to do outside work. When I came to America, I never believed I would have to go to work outside of my home. But look what happened! My husband made a meager living, so what are children for if not to help their parents. I realized that my son, Carlo, would not be able to help till the age of 12, for that was in 1901 when a boy could not get working papers unless he was that old. I hoped Jennie, my oldest daughter, would help me. But no, they changed the law and Jennie had to go to school till she was 14. Thank God, I managed to squeeze out a day here and there so that Jennie could stay home and work on pieces of embroidery, which was well paid for by—[name of firm]. I was lucky the school inspector [a truant officer] was a nice man.[91]

In 1910, another immigrant recalled that in his uncle's restaurant in Little Italy, his wife and their children were needed to work in the family business, so he took his daughter out of school.

Josephine, the girl, helped a great deal though she was only eight years old. As a matter of fact, she did more work than her brother, Nick, who was fourteen years old. When Josephine was ten years old, the father forbade her to go to school. In his estimation, she could read and write, and that was enough for any Italian girl. The father insisted that she was big enough to give real help to her parents. Nickey, the boy was encouraged to go to school but he was expected also to work in the father's restaurant.[92]

In the 1920s, Linda Tarabori's education was also interrupted for financial reasons. Although she eventually graduated from high school, she was not able to go to college. Her story is as follows:

I only had two years of high school at the time, because we were six children and my father was the only working, but by the time I got in high school, my older sister was working and things were a little bit better. Everything was a little bit better and then I went to Crane High School and completed—got a diploma for a four-year high school, but I remember he wanted to send my oldest brother—my younger brother to college and he didn't want to go.[93]

In all these accounts, only the female children were taken out of school to help the family economically. The Old World notion that a daughter's place is at home helping her mother is also present here in the first two accounts. In the second account, the daughter at ten was considered physically mature and literate enough to begin her training in the adult world. In a third account, Linda was able to complete high school, but this may not have been the norm for Italian girls or boys.

For instance, Therese Giannetti, who attended high school in the 1930s, stated:

I went to high school against protest. . . . You didn't need an education because eventually you're going to get married and have little ones to take care of. There was no such thing as being married and going to work. Forget it. There was no such thing. I was determined to get an education. I fought tooth and nail and I went. . . . Out of seven children, I was the only one who went and graduated from high school. My brothers didn't want to go. They had a choice to go and they didn't want to go.[94]

However, Dante A. Greco, who attended high school in the 1940s, thought it was unusual for his father to encourage him and his sister to graduate high school. He stated:

I can recall my father was pretty adamant about wanting an education for my sister and I. And from when I was 7 or 8 years old, he always used to say, "You're going to go to college." I used to tell him, "Well, gee, dad, you know, what if I'm not smart enough?" He said, "You will be, as long as you keep studying." You know, and it was—it was almost an obsession with him. . . . I think his position was unique in that he wanted us to go to school. A lot of others felt that the kids should get out and work as soon as possible, because it was a source of income and obviously in those days, every dollar counted and if a person was strong enough to work, that's what he should be doing. This was the thinking of most of the Italian people at the time, but I thought my dad was unique in that he felt an education was much more important in the long run than going to work right away.[95]

Lastly, Sam Ori, who also attended high school in the 1940s, was one of the kids that Dante was referring to in his account. Sam said:

I did not graduate high school, because my father wanted me to go to work. It's a hard thing to say, to explain this, because he didn't believe in too much schooling. He figured I was already 17 years old and what am I doing in school when I should be working. So, this is the old country way, but over there, they went to work when they were 13, 12, years old. So, he couldn't see this. So, he complained, complained, complained. And I wasn't doing that great in school either, but it was just the idea of trying to get the diploma. Well, okay, I quit school. I went to work for a construction outfit, Meyer's construction.[96]

Daughters in particular had responsibilities in the home, which took precedence over all other activities including school. These responsibilities included caring for a sick parent or marriage. In the 1930s, Florence Roselli, an Italian Chicagoan, was expected to drop out of school because her father was ill, but she had to help send her younger brother to college.

They [her parents] felt that I should have gone beyond high school, but it was at this point that my father became very ill and I, so then I didn't go beyond high school . . . he and my older brother and I say helped, and my mother, helped my younger brother get his college education.[97]

After Florence's obligations to her family were met, she was able to finish high school and go to college until she got married and had to drop out of school again. She continued:

And as I look back now, I never ceased wanting to go to school myself, but I married and had two children and then the first responsibility was to educate your own children.[98]

After her children became adults, thus fulfilling her family obligations, Florence was able to return to school once more. She said:

And so I started college again when I was in my forties. I worked as a part time librarian at Elmhurst Public Library, and did all of my undergraduate work, took me twelve years, but I enjoyed every minute of it.[99]

She later became a teacher and eventually pursued a master's degree in library science.

Another example, Rose Clementi, who was born in Chicago in 1909, was allowed to attend school although her mother was sick, because the school was able to accommodate her. However, she was expected to drop out of school when she got married. Rose's story is as follows:

And when I was going to school also before I graduated, my mother was very sick for many times. And she had pneumonia and she had pleurisy and very sick, you know. And I used to have to go . . . The teachers were so good to me. They let me go every four hours . . . whenever the time for her medicine . . . I'd leave the school . . . 'cause we lived across the street from the school. I'd leave the school. They'd give me permission to go home and give her her medicine.[100]

At age fourteen, Rose was married and she was supposed to drop out of school. However, school age had been extended to sixteen and her sister tried unsuccessfully to bribe the truant officer. This time Rose's husband had to accommodate her or face six months jail time or a $125 fine. She said:

And my husband had to agree that I'd go to school after we were married . . . one day a week. One day a week, every Monday. I looked forward to that Monday. I just enjoyed that school. I wanted to go to school. I didn't want to be married.[101]

Knowing that she would have to drop out of school when she became pregnant at age sixteen, she hid her pregnancy. Rose explained that she felt more of an obligation to her volleyball team and did not want to quit in the middle of the season. She said:

I was the captain of the volleyball team there . . . and jumping around the gym and all of that. And I was pregnant. But I never told anyone. No one knew I was pregnant. And I'd be putting on a garment every Monday morning. I'd put that on tight, and tighten myself up. And when I'd come home I'd be blue in the face.[102]

By the mid twentieth century, there is evidence that at least one Italian immigrant parent discarded cultural dictates and saw the value of schooling for her daughter. In 1957, an SGA counselor reported that an Italian girl was scolded by her mother for the "D" on her most recent grade report and that her mother was upset by the failing grades from her past grade reports.[103] Furthermore, her mother was angry that the girl decided to drop out of school and work full time. She was even upset that her daughter did not bother to save any money from her job for tuition for the next term. This particular mother cared about her daughter's achievement or success in school. The fact that she expressed concern that her daughter did not save money for tuition for the next term and her efforts to seek financial assistance in the form of an SGA scholarship indicated that mother probably intended for her daughter to graduate high school.

Lastly, some Italian immigrants were just as concerned with the practicality of schooling and the dangers of mixed education as they were in their homeland. During the 1920s when vocational curriculum was stressed in the high schools, this was a popular scenario: A. (a girl) quit school at fourteen and went to work in a dress shop. B. studied dressmaking for three years in high school. After a total of four years of schooling, B. only earns $22 and A. earns $30. And all B. knows she learned from A.[104]

Moreover, in the 1920s, Italian Americans also tried to preserve their daughters' chastity and did not want their daughters to attend coed schools. Dominic Pandolfi remembered:

Girls, of course, when I went to high school, my sister went to high school and the Italians were very protective about their daughters. It was just unheard of to send her off to go two miles to high school and mixed education. My sister went, the third sister; the second one when she graduated eighth grade she went to business school. She was typing and things like that. My older sister took the place of mother, mother's helper. When she graduated or finished seventh grade she was her assistant.[105]

Immigrant fathers refused to send their daughters to night school to learn English even with the reassurance that the classes would be restricted to females and would be taught by women.[106] This concern over mixed schooling was a cultural belief brought to America from Italy.

Polish Catholic Attitudes and Schooling Experiences in Poland

Between 1900 and 1918, Poland was dominated by three countries: Prussia, Russia, and Austria. Each country instituted its own educational policies for the area of its domination. All of them incorporated assimilation as part of the education process.[107] However, Polish people secretly taught Polish language, history, and Catholicism at home.[108] Poland became a free state in 1918.[109] By February 1919, free education was available for all children seven to fourteen years old. Article 118 of the Constitution of 1921 and the Constitution of 1935 made elementary education compulsory for all citizens.[110] However, there were no provisions made for facilities, teachers, or textbooks.[111] Although, there was no official policy specifically regarding the education of girls, accounts from Polish people indicate that parental attitudes, the need for child labor, the ability to pay, and religion determined whether a child received schooling. Sometimes all these reasons were used to deter children from going to school.

In 1898, a Polish man wrote a letter to the newspaper describing his father's attitude toward education. He wrote:

> Until 10 years of age I did not know the alphabet, or, exactly speaking, I knew only the letter B. Father did not send me to school. He always used to repeat: "We have grown old and we cannot read nor write, yet we live. So you, my children, will also live without knowledge."[112]

His father did not think it was necessary for his survival to go to school. Another reason his father did not send him to school was because he needed him to work around the farm. The man continued:

> Once my mother took me to church. I looked to the right; a boy smaller than myself was praying from a book. I looked to the left; an-

other one just like the first held a book, and I stood between them like a ninny. I went home and told my father that I would learn from a book. My father scolded me: "And who will peel potatoes in the winter and pasture the geese in summer?"[113]

Still yet another reason his father would not let him learn to read was that it could damn his soul to hell. The Polish man wrote:

Once while peeling potatoes, I escaped from my father and went to an old man who knew not only how to read, but how to write well. I asked him to show me [letters] on the primer, and he did not refuse. . . . Father showered a few strokes on me and said: "Snotty fellow, don't you know that, as the old people say, whoever learns written stuff casts himself into hell?"[114]

Similarly in Austria-dominated Poland, Victoria Majerski was kept from school first for child care, then for religious reasons. Her experiences occurred in 1907. She said:

We were very small then. . . . I was only eight years old and my brother was only one year old. I take care of him when my mother went to work. That's why I get no school.[115]

Her mother needed her labor at home as a babysitter. Then her mother used religion to keep her out of school. She said:

And my mother was Catholic. Oh boy, that came before anything. And my stepfather he wants me to go [to school]. "Send her. Send her." But my mother wouldn't let me.[116]

The school was Lutheran, but she did not get a chance to go to Catholic school either. Her parents thought she was too big. She did not resist because she felt embarrassed that she was taller than the other children. She remembered:

There was one winter in a school in Poland. Then after that, they won't send me, but I was a bigger girl . . . the little kids, you know I don't want it. That's why I don't get much school over there.[117]

Evidence shows that there was some support for education. In Russia-dominated Poland, some parents saw education as a way to resist subordination. Martha Leszcyk, who immigrated to the United States in 1906 at the age of one, stated:

And the Russians, they didn't want Polish people to send their children to school, they wanted them to be, just because, when a person has no education, he will never ask for something more, ask for something that belongs to him.[118]

In 1914, one Polish woman wrote a letter to her sister in which she rejected reasons that some women used against educating children. She wrote:

Our women don't care for kindergartens and schools, they pass indifferently by the consumers' shops. We are angry with our husbands and sons when they spend money for papers and books, and often we don't send our children to school and we keep them home for any trifling reason, for the sake of some work which somebody else could do. If our son or daughter wants to go to a farm school, we withhold them because there is work at home and we pretend that we have no money.[119]

She lists the need for child labor as a reason people don't send their children to school. However, she does not believe that it is a legitimate reason, but an excuse. She looked down upon the women's reluctance to invest in learning by not purchasing reading materials and sending their children to farm school to learn modern agricultural methods.

Polish Catholic Attitudes and Schooling Experiences in the United States

Because of the American Home Economics Association's (AHEA) Save the Family Campaign in 1908, home economic courses were introduced in American schools. Home economics was intended to be the female counterpart to industrial education, which was generally thought of as a male vocational feature of the high school curriculum.[120] The home economics courses offered at American high schools were harmonious to a certain extent with the type of education Polish immigrants typically wanted for their daughters. However, there was some conflict regarding whether the high school course was necessary since the mother usually taught these skills at home. Some of the mothers disagreed with the methods of homemaking that their daughters were taught.

Polish immigrant parents and American schools believed that education for girls should emphasize the care of children and the home. The home economics courses typically offered were housekeeping, cooking, sewing, household economics, nourishment, family relations, and personal hygiene.[121] For those entering the workforce, the type of jobs they were trained for (garment industry, domestic servants, and cooks) were rooted in home economics.[122]

Polish immigrant mothers taught their daughters the same skills at home. In 1929, Marie S. from Nanticoke, Pennsylvania, was asked to leave school to help her mother with the younger children, to perform household chores, and to earn an income by sewing.[123] These were the same types of activities that she would have been doing had she stayed in school.

Similarly Anna S.'s father encouraged her to drop out of school to help raise her brothers and to sew.[124] Arlene G., from Nanticoke, Pennsylvania, left school early so she could work in the family store.[125] Her duties included killing and cleaning the chickens that were for sale.[126]

Regardless of where they learned them—in school or in the home—all the girls learned skills related to the care and management of the household, such as raising children, performing chores, and preparing food. Just like their immigrant mothers, these Polish daughters were also taught to sew or trained to work in the family business—jobs that would allow them to earn money without leaving home.

Moreover, some parents disagreed with the methods of the high school course. They wondered why they should send their daughters to school when they could learn the same things at home.[127] In addition, school courses were textbook based. Teachers assigned homework from these books, which disrupted home life. One mother remarked that her daughter "leaves the housework for me to do and sits reading a book."[128] Later she said, "D. doesn't care for company. She wants to keep a book before her eyes—she is just like her father. I can't stand her."[129]

Still, there is some evidence that demonstrates support of formal schooling. According to Emma A. Kowalenko, Polish Americans in particular saw education as a way to preserve their identity. She wrote:

A mother's duty consisted also of giving, encouraging, and seeking an education for herself. An undereducated mother could not be an adequate teacher. She was expected to teach language, history, and patriotism—preserve Polishness.[130]

One way Polish American women of Chicago used education to preserve Polishness was by supporting Polish Catholic high schools and universities that offered courses in Polish language and history.

Across the country in cities such as Plymouth and Nanticoke, Pennsylvania, Polish and Slovak immigrants identified the sickness or the death or a parent as reasons for their truancy in their narratives. Frances B. from Plymouth, Pennsylvania, and her sisters left school after the eighth grade in order to make dresses at home because her father broke his back and her mother became mentally ill.[131] Helen G., a Slovak, never attended school but entered a garment factory after the death of her parents.[132] After Lillian N.'s father died, she left school to sell milk to help support herself and nine brothers and sisters.[133]

By the 1920s there was some change in these practices. Martha Leszcyk was allowed to attend high school in Chicago, but she was not able to go to college because her mother was sick. She said:

> I was the only one that finished just the high school. I didn't go any higher, but I stayed home and my mother was very sick. . . . But you know I didn't attend that much because my mother was very sickly . . . though my brother was the eldest naturally he wouldn't pitch in and stuff like that.[134]

It was the daughter's duty to take care of a sick parent. Martha was able to go further in school than the others. The compulsory education age was raised to sixteen by the time she entered high school.

Financial hardship in the 1930s was given as reason for keeping Polish Catholic girls out of school. Because public school was not considered an option for them, religion played a role in keeping girls out of school just as it did in Poland. For example, Mary Janka said:

> You must remember that I graduated in the peak of the Depression . . . from grammar school . . . 1932. He [her father] always felt bad that he couldn't send me to a four-year course in high school. I went to St. Sylvester's because it was of walking distance from here and the tuition was $33.00 a year . . . $33.00 a year. That he could afford, yea.[135]

Virginia Martell tried to attend public school in 1935, but she encountered some resistance from the Catholic community. She said:

> I was no longer able to go to Catholic school because that required too much money. I went into a public school. At that time the nuns said, "Don't do that because you're going to become a very bad girl." They tried very hard to try to talk me out of going to public school.[136]

She remained committed to learning. In 1942, she wanted to go back to school as an adult. She was able to go because her husband shared her child-rearing responsibilities. She said:

> My husband always worked but I always wanted to better myself. I kept thinking that someday I would like to go back to school, but how? I only had the one-year of high school when I quit. . . . While he watched the baby in the morning, I would go to school for a half a day. I would come home and he would go to work in the afternoon.[137]

However, she still endured hardships going to school as a mother. She said:

> It took me a year to go to school but I knew I could not fail. I studied very hard. Between doing diapers and steaming bottles, and taking care of the baby, I would try to study very hard because I couldn't fail.[138]

The lack of encouragement by school officials was also a reason for truancy. During the Progressive era of social efficiency, Chicago schools employed psychotherapists to place people in professions. Psychotherapists from the Bureau of Child Study using a battery of physical, psychological, and achievement tests recommended courses of study. One girl, who was a straight-A student, was diagnosed as "having a compensating need for achievement."[139] She was discouraged from going to college because a "competitive schooling environment or college would be disastrous."[140]

In addition, the socialization of Polish children by their parents stressed the importance of work as a part of their preparation for adulthood. However, children were not encouraged to work for individual gain or for social mobility. Instead, all wage-earning family members were expected to contribute all of their earnings into a communal pot to be used for the well-being of the entire family.

Polish parents either collected their children's paychecks individually or collected the paychecks of the entire family all at once.[141] In this way, children were preparing for adulthood by helping to take care of a family.

Irish Attitudes and Schooling Experiences in Ireland

Historian Walter Bronwen claimed that in 1891 Irish girls received more education than boys because they were not able to inherit land and this would provide them with skills so that they would be able to better support the family from abroad.[142] For those remaining in Ireland, the Irish Education Act of 1892 made attendance compulsory for boys and girls.[143] However, the purpose of educating girls was to make them better wives. Moreover, class distinctions limited the amount of schooling beyond primary education. Historian Maria Luddy wrote:

> Women's role was in the domestic sphere, and the care of children and husbands; cooking and cleaning did not, it was thought require vast educational knowledge. Women were considered naturally inferior to men and their intellectual abilities less capable of development.[144]

Girls were taught needlework and skills needed in the home.[145] Middle-class Irish girls received a more intellectual education, but they were also prepared to be wives and mothers.[146] Although Irish women were receiving university degrees throughout the 1890s, they were still treated as intellectually inferior to men. Women were not allowed to be professors. For example, Mary Hayden was a recipient of the Junior Fellowship in the Royal University in Dublin.[147] However, her fellowship was in name only. Had she been a male, she would have been entitled to lecture in history at the University.[148] Another Irish woman, Hanna Shechy, earned a master's degree in French and won the Gold Medal, a prestigious academic award.[149] Her husband resigned as registrar at the Royal University over the nonrecognition of women graduates.[150]

In the 1930s, state policy reaffirmed the place of women in the home. Bishop Morrisroe of Achnory stated in 1931:

Upon the stouter shoulders devolves the task of winning by toil what is needed for the upkeep of the household, while to the weaker member belongs the duty of applying the resources to needs as they arise. In this way each partner has a separate sphere of activity. . . . The observance of neatness, tidiness, and orderliness in the house, coupled with the supervision of things destined for the table, will entitle the housewife to golden opinions, while a sympathetic word to the breadwinner after his day's toil will give the humblest meal a delicious flavor.[151]

In 1937, the constitution offered family allowances "to ensure that mothers shall not be obliged by economic necessity to engage in labor to the neglect of their duties in the home."[152] This provision resulted in the exclusion of mothers but not childless wives from the workforce.[153] This attitude was also reflected in the attitudes of Irish women toward education.

Mary Coleum wrote in 1947 that when she wanted to attend college to prepare herself for a job, her female relatives were against the idea.

What female relatives I have were against the scheme [her going to college] and considered that a suitable arranged marriage would be better security for my future, but the men of the family even my grandfather, were strongly for the four years' training in Dublin.[154]

Another woman, Audrey, who attended a convent school in Ireland during the 1950s, remembered that her education taught her to be subordinate and to prepare herself for marriage. She said:

We were supposed to model ourselves on the Blessed Virgin Mary, to have good Christian Catholic values and to be a good wife. I recently picked up an old Victorian book at an auction, and it was about how to prepare a young lady for marriage and all the things she was expected to do. And I didn't see much difference between what it was saying and what we were told in the 1950s in that dreadful convent I was in![155]

She also commented on her courses. She said:

We had no skills whatever. I didn't even learn domestic subjects because I did music. If you were not going to the University—and we didn't see the point—there was no emphasis on a career for a girl at all.[156]

According to another woman's account from the 1950s, teachers did not expect that female students would go to the university either. She recalled:

> It was expected that you'd be going nowhere [except] to marriage. I had no intentions of ever getting married and I think that's why so many people emigrated to America.[157]

Although women were being prepared for marriage in the 1950s, there were not that many marriages taking place because of the depression in Ireland.[158] Eimear, who was born in 1942 in Ireland to a middle-class family, commented:

> There wasn't any marriages taking place at the time. I was the up and coming generation that would be leaving. It was just an understood thing that anyone that reached seventeen, eighteen did two things— they either went to England or they went to America. The majority of people would go to England, unless you were fortunate enough to have somebody sponsor you to the States.[159]

Mary Walsh, who was born in 1937, immigrated to the United States in the 1950s for educational opportunities. She was able to attend primary school in Ireland, but she had to help around the farm because her father became ill. She said:

> My father was sick, so I was kept from school for that reason. My mother felt that was an injustice so when a cousin came home and visited she gave me the opportunity of going to America. . . . I actually thought hey, without an education where do you go from there? This was the first real opportunity and I felt I'd try it anyway; I won't let it go by.[160]

When she arrived in America, she did not go to school. She worked six days a week taking care of four children. Eventually, she got married and had children of her own.[161]

Another Irish woman, Frances Newall Coen, who was born in 1937, also immigrated to the United States in the 1950s. She described her schooling experiences in Ireland in these terms:

> Education wasn't free. It was a pound or two pounds every three months for secondary school. Most people didn't have the opportunity to go to secondary school because they simply couldn't have the

money. I was robbed of that. . . . You didn't get the opportunity. You also didn't get the encouragement from your parents because before them they had the same background. There was no one to tell you it's important. To be honest with you I think most of my education is in the United States.[162]

This account was similar to the experiences of Jewish, Italian, and Polish women from working-class families. They were also deprived of education beyond what was compulsory for financial reasons.

Frances also mentioned that class distinctions affected her experiences at school as well. She said:

I resented the class distinction in Ireland. I feel that it marked a lot of us, and I was one. I was able to overcome it but in school we were taught by sisters we were not important as people. My work in school was not important, but the lawyer's daughter was important. They were all in the front of the class. They were the people picked to stand in front of the class and read their compositions.[163]

Anne, who attended a rural national school in Ireland during the 1950s, had a similar experience. She said:

My father worked in a shop and my friend's father was a carpenter. The other girls' fathers were posher, and the snobby element was there. They got away with murder and we got murdered for it.[164]

The attitude that school was supposed to prepare girls for marriage was consistent from 1900 to 1950. Girls who were able to attend secondary schools were also taught how to be wives. Those women who were able to earn university degrees were not able to find jobs as scholars because women were perceived to be less intelligent than men.

Irish Catholic Attitudes and Schooling Experiences in the United States

The schooling experiences of Irish Catholics in the United States were different from Jewish, Italian, and Polish immigrant groups in the 1900s because they were already a settled group. Moreover, they had a history of academic achievement in the United States. There also was a notable change in the attitude toward the education of women in the United States compared to Ireland. This was possibly due to acculturation.

While other immigrants, such as Jews, Italians, and Poles, were coming to America in large droves between 1900 and 1910, Irish immigration tapered off. The major Irish immigration occurred between 1870 and 1900.[165] In fact in 1981, Andrew M. Greeley, an Irish American historian, asserted that

> three-quarters of us came after the Famine immigration, two-thirds of us came before the twentieth century, and all but seven percent of us came before the end of the Irish civil war in 1923.[166]

By the 1900s a second generation of Irish Americans had reached adulthood. The Irish were also different from the other groups because they were English speaking and educated. According to Greeley, 75 percent of Irish Americans in 1981 had parents who were educated in the national schools and could read, write, and speak English fluently.[167]

Irish Americans were also educating their children beyond the elementary level. In 1907, their college attendance rate was above the national average.[168] By 1910, the Irish were choosing managerial and professional careers at a higher than average rate.[169] Irish women were included.

The attitude of the proper role of Irish Catholic women as wives and mothers did not hinder their academic success and employment opportunities in America as it did in Ireland.[170] Irish American women had a history of academic success dating back to the late nineteenth century. Andrew Greeley stated that his grandmother, who lived in Chicago in 1880, had more education than his grandfather did when they met. He noted:

> My schoolteacher grandmother, born of immigrants in London, was better educated and probably of a better social ranking (a not unusual situation in immigrant groups, since limited upward mobility was more readily available to women than to men at certain stages in the immigration experience) [than his grandfather].[171]

According to Margaret Haley, Irish immigrant mothers in the nineteenth century encouraged their daughters to go to school.

Haley stated that her mother valued education "as only the Irish, who had been denied the full measure of education, could value it."[172] Her mother also encouraged her to become a teacher. She told her to "educate, in order that your children may be free."[173]

As early as 1876, nuns encouraged Irish American children to pursue their education beyond the elementary level.[174] They also recruited young girls for their own religious communities. Girls who became nuns were also trained to be nurses or teachers.[175] By the 1920s, an estimated 70 percent of Chicago's public school teachers were graduates of Catholic secondary schools.[176] The majority of them were Irish.[177]

Irish American women also pursued careers in law and politics. For example, Mary O'Toole graduated from Washington College of Law in 1908.[178] In August 1921, she became the first woman appointed as a judge in the Municipal Court of the District of Columbia.[179] Helen P. McCormick also made her mark in law. After graduating from Brooklyn Law School in 1913, she became the first woman appointed as assistant district attorney in New York on December 1, 1917.[180] The first woman to be appointed magistrate in the State of New York in 1919 was an Irish American woman, Jean Hortense Norris.[181] In the political arena, Mary T. Norton from New Jersey made history in 1924 as the first woman to be elected to the House of Representatives from the Eastern part of the United States.[182] These feats would not have been possible for women in Ireland at this time.

Nationally, educational opportunities for Irish American women increased in the 1930s throughout the 1950s. Between World Wars I and II, one-fourth of Irish American high school graduates went to college.[183] The majority of them were women.[184] Following World War II, the GI Bill allowed even more Irish Americans to earn their bachelor's degrees as well as graduate and professional degrees.[185]

However, the majority of Irish Americans did not go to college in the 1940s, but college attendance became the norm for Irish Chicagoans in the 1950s. Greeley recalled:

> When I graduated from high school in 1946, only a few of my male classmates, as I remember, only one of the women whom I went to grammar school planned to go to college. Eight years later [1954], when I was ordained and sent to an Irish neighborhood of about the

same cultural and social level as the one in which I had been raised, it was taken for granted that everyone would go to college.[186]

This account suggests that attitudes toward education influenced Irish Americans' decision to go to college more than culture and social class. Given the financial means, Irish American men and women furthered their education.

Conclusion

The accounts given in this chapter were based on the reported experiences of individual women from Jewish, Italian, Polish, and Irish immigrant groups. Their experiences were not necessarily representative of their respective ethnic communities. Nevertheless, it was useful to examine these experiences. They offered a glimpse of what going to school may have been like for them.

There was a degree of consistency in the women's stories. For example, most of the women mentioned limited educational opportunities for them due to gender role expectations. They also remembered that the type of education parents wanted for their daughters centered on the preparation for their future roles as wives and mothers. That idea was transmitted from Europe and survived in America for many years. However, Irish American women by 1900 were able to break from traditional Irish attitudes, which valued educational and occupational achievement more for males than females. Still, most of the stories were remarkably similar, and it appears as though gender differences affected parental attitudes toward school and immigrant female students' schooling experiences in more profound ways than cultural and class differences.

CHAPTER 5

Conclusion

For Italian, Irish, Polish, and Jewish women in Chicago, immigration was an act of both self- and cultural preservation. These women did not leave their native lands just for the pursuit of economic and social advancement. They fled from their war-torn homelands for their own safety and the safety of their families. They were also seeking refuge from cultural imperialism taking place in the public schools and society within their homelands. These reasons as well as issues of access, opportunities, and family expectations at the intersection of gender and ethnicity shaped their attitudes toward Americanization and schooling in the Chicago public school system.

The absence of Italian, Irish, Polish, and Jewish immigrant women from the history of immigrant education was notable since they were key players in the assimilation process from 1900 to 1950. As mothers, they exerted a considerable amount of influence within the home. They were the primary caregivers of children, clothing them as they saw fit and determining which language would be the primary language spoken in the home. They were also in charge of housekeeping and the family diet. They acted as the bearers of tradition, passing customs down from one generation to the next.

The failure to Americanize and assimilate women also hindered the assimilation of the family. Immigrant mothers allowed their children to adopt the behaviors of the dominant American culture while at school, but would not tolerate them within the home. While children were being Americanized at school, they were not allowed to totally accept an American identity at home. Immigrant girls in particular had to learn traditional cultural practices regarding housekeeping and religious rituals. They were also expected to adhere to traditional gender roles assigned to them.

Moreover, the Americanization experiences of immigrant women were different from those of men. Some immigrant women saw Americanization as a public practice. They satisfied laws of the land in public while keeping intact cultural dictates within the privacy of their homes. Their ethnic identity determined who they were as individuals, their roles within their family, and their place with the larger community.

Chicago's Board of Education policies and practices within its public schools acted against the aims of immigrant women for self- and cultural preservation. Chicago's public schools did not adequately address their cultural beliefs and practices regarding the nature and purpose of education for female immigrant students. In addition, policies were enacted without regard to the strength of ethnic bonds of immigrant students. There was no mention of their history in schools, preventing the children of immigrants from learning their heritage. Within public schools, immigrant children were scrutinized and encouraged to reject the fundamental aspects of their identity: language, appearance, cultural norms, and religion.

Still, Americanization programs within public school were not as effective because of parental resistance, which manifested itself in truancy and enrollment in Catholic schools. Catholic schools before the 1950s allowed immigrants to keep their cultures intact by teaching native language, history, and habits. However, some mothers simply kept their daughters at home so that they could be taught the dictates of their culture. Those immigrant female students who remained with the public school system were not able to practice being American at home. After not being accepted as American in schools, they were forced to live in conflict with their mothers for the duration of their formal school years.

Contrary to past historical scholarship, my research reveals that immigrant parents were not against education. They were against public schools, which were acting against the aims of self- and cultural preservation. This was evident in their willingness to support ethnic Catholic schools as long they were teaching the language, culture, and history of their homelands. Moreover, parental beliefs and attitudes toward the education of their children were gender based and culturally rooted in their native homelands. Yet past scholarship overlooked gender, choosing instead to focus on racial and ethnic differences regarding parental attitudes toward school and immigrant children's schooling experiences.

However, the evidence has shown that racial and ethnic differences are obscured when gender is taken into account. Many of the accounts from immigrant females indicated that overriding concerns for cultural preservation caused girls to be withdrawn from schools sometimes against their will in order to prepare them for their traditional gender roles as wives and mothers by serving as helpmates to their mother. In this way, immigrant mothers were also able to resume their roles as teachers to their female children and to pass down cultural traditions and practices to them, thereby realizing their goal of cultural preservation.

Future scholarship on the history of immigrant education should be cautious of statistics and data that do not account for gender. Past research was based on data gathered from male subjects, and therefore generalizations regarding ethnic differences were applicable only to males. Accounts gathered from Irish, Italian, Polish, and Jewish women regarding their educational experiences indicated that there are shared patterns across ethnic groups.

Furthermore, many of the studies done on immigrant attitudes toward education do not take into consideration the lack of opportunities to receive formal education due to politics, social norms, and financial circumstances in both their native countries and in the United States. Historians simply assumed that ethnic groups did not value education when literacy was not widespread.

Historians of immigrant education should focus on the role of women within their families and society. These roles are an indication of the type of education that parents are seeking for their female children. It is not necessarily the same type of education that they would want their male children to undertake. Historians should also be mindful of the societal limitations and cultural expectations that are placed on women. Although these limitations and expectations may have originated within their native homelands, they were transported into the United States and passed down from generation to generation.

Finally, because of the influence that women have on their children in facilitating or hindering the assimilation process taking place within public schools, the schooling experiences and attitudes toward education of female immigrant students warrant more study. For some immigrant women, the Chicago Board of Education goals to Americanize and assimilate were contrary to their goals of preserving their native culture. Furthermore, the type of education offered to immigrant female students, particularly in Little Mothers' classes, were in conflict with how immigrant mothers envisioned their preparation for their roles in life as wife, mother, and bearer of cultural tradition. For immigrant female students, these differences created a source of conflict both at home and at school.

Although there is a significant amount of historical and social science scholarship on ethnic differences in schooling and academic achievement, there is room for further studies that take into account the gendered nature of enculturation, acculturation, and school experiences. Much of the past scholarship on ethnic differences in schooling focuses almost exclusively on cultural values and school experiences. This study has shown that cultural values of education did not differ as greatly among Irish, Polish, Italian, and Jewish women as among Irish, Polish, Italian, and Jewish men. Family expectations for the education of young women also did not differ sharply among ethnic groups. The attitudes of immigrant parents regarding the education of their female children did not change significantly as a consequence of their acculturation in American society.

The findings from this study are important because they provide a gendered interpretation of the immigrant experience, which will alter the way the history of immigrant education is viewed and written. It also brought to light the needs of female immigrant students that should be addressed by the public school system in the interest of providing equal educational opportunities. Although the immigrant groups have changed over time, there are gender-related issues—such as the preparation for the roles as wife and mother, child-rearing practices, the types of jobs that are socially acceptable for women, and the position of women within religion and its relationship to education—that are also culturally based and still present among current immigrant groups.

In fact, questions regarding the impact of cultural beliefs on schooling experiences and attitudes toward education of immigrant groups are currently being addressed by historians of education, with increasing attention given to gender. In light of this and other studies on the impact of ethnicity and immigration in education, it would be a mistake to assume that data collected on immigrant men is representative of the experiences of an entire ethnic group. It is now known that immigrant women have Americanization and schooling experiences that are distinct from those of immigrant men.

The scope of this research can be expanded to include data collected from ethnic museums, Jane Addams's Hull House, and Catholic school records. More oral history interviews of Irish, Polish, Italian, and Jewish women who lived during the 1900–1950 era need to be conducted. Although oral history archives of these ethnic groups already exist in Chicago, each group is not equally represented in terms of the total number of interviews conducted; the number of female interviewees is also limited. The scope of information relating to school experiences, parental expectations, and cultural values concerning education is also inadequate for use by historians of immigrant education.

While the intent of this book is to give voice to Irish, Italian, Polish, and Jewish immigrant women whose stories have been overlooked in the historiography of immigrant education, current policymakers and educational reformers may benefit from these findings and subsequent studies on the historical experiences of immigrant female students. History has shown that educational policies and schooling practices in conflict with parental expectations for the education of their children are doomed to failure.

The women's stories represented here also stressed the need to seek multiple perspectives when developing educational policy. Many educational reforms are developed based on scientific evidence that measures such tangible things as socioeconomic status, test scores, dropout rate, level of educational achievement, and the number of students representing different ethnic groups. As the histories of women from Irish, Jewish, Italian, and Polish ethnic groups indicate, gender can alter statistical outcomes in significant ways. For example, the enrollment in night school classes and high school graduation rates in Chicago during 1900–1950 was high for certain ethnic groups. When numerical data accounted for gender, disparities were exposed. Therefore, educational reformers and policymakers should learn the ways in which gender plays a role in policies aimed at resolving issues such as truancy and high dropout rates.

Moreover, educational reformers should seek the perspectives of parents and students regarding their educational views and expectations. Quantitative studies on educational attainment are limited in determining attitudes or commitment toward education. Educational policies should not be built on cultural deficit models, which seek to compensate for differences in academic achievement by building or strengthening "assets" or values. There is no consensus among all the ethnic groups present within the United States on which values are useful and should be emphasized by schools. The immigrant accounts in this book also indicate that the differences present within an ethnic group are greater than differences across ethnic groups. Therefore, educational reformers and policymakers should concentrate their efforts on creating educational opportunities for all students.

In addition, the histories presented in this book show that factors beside cultural differences influence school achievement, such as class, language difficulties, racism, perceptions regarding future opportunities, and lack of resources. Moreover, contemporary reformers can implement better programs by asking for input from parents and students within their schools and by studying past experiences of people within similar programs. Recent reforms in Chicago, for example, include offering evening classes for high school students who are truant so that they can catch up in their studies. However, the effectiveness of these programs is questionable.

Historical accounts point out that evening schools are difficult for female students to attend because of child-rearing responsibilities for siblings or their own children, after-school jobs, and familial obligations such as chores or caring for a sick parent. These programs could have accounted for these circumstances had the educational reformers and policymakers looked at historical experiences of female students attending evening classes.

By understanding how gender affects the history of immigrant education and by using educational history to inform current educational policies and practices, better educational programs will be developed that fit the actual needs of students within modern public schools.

Notes

Chapter One

1. Carl N. Degler, "Is There a History of Women?" An inaugural lecture delivered before Oxford University on 14 March 1974 (Oxford: Oxford University Press, 1975), 8.

2. They were also inadvertently excluding women. In the preface to *The New Immigration* (New York: Macmillan, 1913), Peter Roberts wrote: "This book is an attempt to describe the quality, the industrial efficiency, the social life, and the relation to the native-born of the men of the new immigration. . . . [By] the [term] 'new immigration' is meant the people emigrating to America from the countries of southeastern Europe; . . . the term 'old immigration' is applied to men emigrating from northwestern Europe." For examples of authors using data on men to describe both men and women as a group, see David K. Cohen, "Immigrants and the Schools," *Review of Educational Research* 40 (1970): 13–27; Timothy L. Smith, "Immigrant Social Aspirations and American Education, 1880–1930," *American Quarterly* 21 (1969): 523–543; Leonard Dinnerstein, "Education and the Advancement of American Jews," in A*merican Education and the European Immigrant: 1840–1940*, ed. Bernard J. Weiss (Urbana: University of Illinois Press, 1982), 44–60.

3. Helena Znaniecka Lopato, *Polish Americans* (New Brunswick, NJ: Transaction Publishers, 1994), 91ff, 246; Thomas Kessner, *The Golden Door: Italian and Jewish Mobility in New York City 1880–1915* (New York: Oxford University Press, 1977), 84.

4. Joel Perlmann, *Ethnic Differences: Schooling and Social Structure among the Irish, Italians, Jews, and Blacks in an American City,*

1880–1935 (New York: Cambridge University Press, 1988); Howard Weisz, *Irish-American and Italian-American Educational Views, 1870–1900: A Comparison* (New York: Arno Press, 1976).

5. Perlmann, 53.
6. Ibid.
7. Kerby Miller, *Irish Popular Culture, 1650–1850* (Ballsbridge, Ireland: Irish Academic Press, 1999).
8. Tom Ireland, *Ireland, Past and Present* (New York: G. P. Putnam's Sons, 1942), 139; Stephen Bryne, *Irish Emigration to the United States* (New York: Arno Press and the New York Times, 1969), 42.
9. Ireland, 184–185, 252–253; David Fitzpatrick, *The Two Irelands 1912–1939* (Oxford: Oxford University Press, 1998), 16–17, 192–195.
10. Perlmann, 53.
11. Charles Townshend, *Ireland: The Twentieth Century* (London: Arnold, 1998), 11.
12. Ibid.
13. Ibid., 12.
14. Maria Luddy, *Women in Ireland, 1800–1918* (Cork, Ireland: Cork University Press, 1995), 90.
15. Ibid.
16. Perlmann, 53.
17. Case Histories 4–50, Immigrant Protective League, UIC Special Collections; Virginia Martell—106, Oral History Archives of Chicago Polonia, CHS Manuscripts and Archives; Dominic Pandolfi—27, Italian Oral History Project, UIC Special Collections.
18. Margaret MacCurtain and Donneha O'Corrain, *Women in Irish Society* (Westport, CT: Greenwood Press, 1979), 47; Jenny Beale, *Women in Ireland* (Bloomington: Indiana University Press, 1987), 130; Ide O'Carroll, *Models for Movers: Irish Women's Emigration to America* (Dublin: Attic Press, 1990), 74.
19. Perlmann, 55–56.
20. Ellen Skerrett, "The Catholic Dimension," in *The Irish in Chicago,* ed. Lawrence J. McCaffrey, Ellen Skerrett, Michael F. Funchion, and Charles Fanning (Urbana: University of Illinois, 1987), 45.
21. Ibid.
22. Weisz, 36.
23. Ibid.
24. Weisz, 218–219.
25. Ibid., 240.
26. Ibid., 262–63.
27. Ibid., 251.
28. Perlmann, 121; Leonard Covello, *The Social Background of the Italo-American School Child* (Leiden, The Netherlands: E. J. Brill, 1967), 287.

29. Covello, 287.
30. Kessner, 40.
31. Kessner, 85.
32. Therese Giannetti—55, Italian American Oral History Project, UIC Special Collections.
33. Rosamond Mirabella—69, Italian American Oral History Project, UIC Special Collections.
34. Ibid.
35. Dante A. Greco—67, Italian American Oral History Project, UIC Special Collections.
36. Humbert S. Nelli, *From Immigrants to Ethnics: The Italian Americans* (New York: Oxford University Press, 1983), 146.
37. Christopher Howard Edson, "Immigrant Perspectives on Work and Schooling: Eastern European Jews and Southern Italians, 1880–1920," Ph.D. dissertation, Stanford University, 1979, 320.
38. Covello, 321.
39. Qtd. in Kessner, 95.
40. Dominic Pandolfi—28, Italian American Oral History Project, UIC Special Collections.
41. Covello, 321.
42. Annual Report of the Board of Education of the City of Chicago, 1911–1912; Annual Report of the Board of Education of the City of Chicago, 1917–1918.
43. Nelli, 144.
44. Perlmann, 91.
45. Kessner, 95. See also Weisz, 409.
46. Florence Rosetti—44, Italian American Oral History Project, UIC Special Collections.
47. Ibid.
48. Ibid.
49. Dorota Praszalowicz, "The Cultural Changes of Polish-American Parochial Schools in Milwaukee, 1866–1988," *Journal of American Ethnic History* (Summer 1994): 23.
50. Ibid.
51. Irwin T. Sanders and Ewa T. Morawska, *Polish-American Community Life: A Survey of Research.* The Community Sociology Monograph Series, vol. 2. Sponsored by Community Sociology Training Program Department of Sociology (Boston: Boston University, and Polish Institute of Arts and Sciences in America, Inc., 1975), 43.
52. Ibid., 44.
53. Ibid., 45.
54. Ibid.
55. Lopato, 147. See also Michael Murray, *Poland's Progress 1919–1939* (London: Orbis, 1945), 113, 209.

56. Ibid.

57. Victoria Majerski—88, Oral History Archives of Chicago Polonia, CHS Manuscripts and Archives.

58. Praszalowicz, 27, 30–31. See also Lopato, 63.

59. Ibid., 24–26.

60. Ibid., 30–31.

61. Mary Janka—116, Oral History Archives of Chicago Polonia, CHS Manuscripts and Archives.

62. Virginia Martell—106, Oral History Archives of Chicago Polonia, CHS Manuscripts and Archives.

63. Lopato, 91; John Bodnar, "Schooling and the Slavic-American Family, 1900–1940," in *American Education and the European Immigrant: 1840–1940*, ed. Bernard J. Weiss (Urbana: University of Illinois Press, 1982), 82.

64. Lopato, 91, 246.

65. Bodnar, 82.

66. Ibid.

67. Ibid.

68. Interview, 3 November 1933, United Charities, CHS Manuscripts and Archives.

69. Kessner, 96–97.

70. Kessner, 97–98.

71. Anuta Sharrow, "Anuta Sharrow," in *Jewish Grandmothers*, eds. Sydelle Kramer and Jenny Masur (Boston: Beacon Press, 1976), 82–83. Hereafter cited as Sharrow.

72. Ibid., 64.

73. Beatrice C. Baskerville, *The Polish Jew* (London: Chapman and Hall, 1906), 83.

74. Ibid., 82.

75. Dinnerstein, 44–45.

76. Fannie Shapiro, "Fannie Shapiro," in *Jewish Grandmothers*, eds. Sydelle Kramer and Jenny Masur (Boston: Beacon Press, 1976), 5. Hereafter cited as Shapiro.

77. Ibid.

78. Kessner, 98.

79. Ibid.

80. Perlmann, 148.

81. Ibid.

82. Ibid.

83. Annual Meeting Reports for the Years 1920–1924. Scholarship and Guidance Association, Chicago, Illinois, UIC Special Collections; Vocational Supervision League Report of Scholarship Work, September 1920–June 1921, Scholarship and Guidance Association, UIC Special Collections.

84. Mollie Linker, "Mollie Linker," in *Jewish Grandmothers*, eds. Sydelle Kramer and Jenny Masur (Boston: Beacon Press, 1976), 94. Hereafter cited as Linker.

85. Abraham J. Karp, *Golden Door to America: The Jewish Immigrant Experience* (New York: The Viking Press, 1976); Stephan F. Brumberg, *Going to America, Going to School: The Jewish Immigrant Public School Encounter in Turn-of-the-Century New York City* (New York: Praeger Publishers, 1986). See also Perlmann, 161.

86. Karp, 179.

87. Frank D. Loomis, *Americanization in Chicago, The Report of a Survey* (Chicago: Chicago Community Trust, 1920), 22–23; Annual Report of the General Superintendent of the Chicago Public Schools, 1918–1919.

88. Shapiro, 11.

89. Psychiatric and Physical Report 1–4, 12 August 1958, Scholarship and Guidance Association, UIC Special Collections.

90. Neil M. Cowan and Ruth Schwartz Cowan, *Our Parents' Lives* (New Brunswick, NJ: Rutgers University Press, 1989), 92.

Chapter 2

1. Lorraine M. McDonnell and Paul T. Hill, *Newcomers in American Schools: Meeting the Educational Needs of Immigrant Youth* (Santa Monica: Rand, 1993), 1.

2. 61st Congress, 3rd Session, Reports of the Immigration Commission, *The Children of Immigrants in Schools*, vol. 2 (Metuchen, NJ: Scarecrow Reprint Corporation, 1970).

3. Loomis, 22–23.

4. Ibid.

5. Ibid.

6. James R. Barrett and David Roediger, "Inbetween Peoples: Race, Nationality, and the New Immigrant Working Class," in *Majority and Minority: The Dynamics of Race and Ethnicity in American Life*, ed. Norman R. Yetman (Boston: Allyn and Bacon, 1999), 151.

7. Judith Cassai—109, Oral History Archives of Chicago Polonia, Chicago Historical Society, Manuscripts and Archives, Chicago, Illinois; hereafter referred to as CHS Manuscripts and Archives.

8. Loomis, 22. Loomis does not list enrollment by ethnicity.

9. Ibid.

10. Ibid. The actual numbers of men and women enrolled in factory classes were not available. Loomis mentioned that the factory classes were attended by "mostly men" in his survey.

11. Ibid.

12. Ibid.; see also Annual Report of the General Superintendent of the Chicago Public Schools, 1918–1919. The school census data listed in the Annual Report do not report the enrollment and attendance of immigrants in night schools separately from native-born students. The night school enrollment for 1920 was not listed, but the enrollment for 1918–1919 school year was available and listed by gender. There were 13,749 men and 13,468 women attending evening school in 1918–1919. It is not known how many of those students were immigrants because both native-born and immigrant students were able to enroll in night school courses. The ethnicities of the students were also not available.

13. Annual Report of the General Superintendent of the Chicago Public Schools, 1918–1919.

14. Ibid.

15. Loomis, 23.

16. Judith Cassai—109.

17. Linker, 102.

18. Shapiro, 11.

19. Chicago Board of Education, A Year of Americanization Work, July 1918–July 1919, Chicago, Illinois.

20. Janet Calvo, "Spouse-Based Immigration Laws: The Legacy of Coverture," in Critical Race Feminism, ed. Adrien Katherine Wing (New York: New York University Press, 1997): 382–383.

21. Ibid.

22. Shapiro, 12–13.

23. Ibid.

24. Case Histories 4–50.

25. Martha Langelan, Back Off! How to Confront and Stop Sexual Harassment and Harassers (New York: Fireside, 1993), 78.

26. Ibid.

27. Maud Nathan, The Story of an Epoch-Making Movement (New York: Doubleday, 1926), 7.

28. Shapiro, 11.

29. Rosa Cohen, Out of the Shadow (New York: George Dovan, 1918), 851.

30. Calvo, 382–383.

31. Ibid.

32. Case Histories 4–50, September 1920–November 1933, Immigrant Protective League, University of Illinois Special Collections, Chicago, Illinois; hereafter referred to as UIC Special Collections.

33. Shapiro, 6.

34. Calvo, 384.

35. Case Histories 4–50.

36. Annual Report, 1930 United Charities.

37. Ibid.

38. Ibid.
39. Carmella Zoppettiti—79, Italian Oral History Project, UIC Special Collections.
40. Kataya Govsky, "Katakya Govsky" in *Jewish Grandmothers,* eds. Sydelle Kramer and Jenny Masur (Boston: Beacon Press, 1976), 70. Hereafter cited as Govsky.
41. Ibid.
42. Ibid.
43. Ibid., 71.
44. Shapiro, 14.
45. Ibid.
46. Ibid.
47. Rose Tellerino—26, Italian Oral History Project, UIC Special Collections.
48. Virginia Martell—106, Oral History Archives of Chicago Polonia, CHS Manuscripts and Archives.
49. Ibid.
50. Dominic Pandolfi—27, Italian Oral History Project, UIC Special Collections.
51. Mary Janka—116, Oral History Archives of Chicago Polonia, CHS Manuscripts and Archives.
52. Ibid.
53. Maria Valiani—80, Italian Oral History Project, UIC Special Collections.
54. Ibid.

Chapter 3

1. Julia Wrigley, *Class, Politics, and Public Schools* (New Brunswick, NJ: Rutgers University Press, 1982), 35, 48.
2. Ibid., 64.
3. Kenneth Finegold, *Experts and Politicians: Reform Challenges to Machine Politics in New York, Cleveland, and Chicago* (Princeton: Princeton University Press, 1995), 164; George S. Counts, *School and Society in Chicago* (New York: Harcourt, Brace & Company, 1928), 266–270.
4. Counts, 268.
5. Annual Report of the Board of Education of the city of Chicago, 1909–1910.
6. In this book, "immigrant children" also refers to children of immigrants.
7. Loomis, 24.
8. Civic education is defined as education for citizenship and character. Chicago Board of Education Education for Citizenship, March 1933, Chicago, Illinois.

9. Ibid.

10. The lesson on people of the countries studied follows a geography lesson. The countries that were studied were not listed. Chicago Board of Education, Education for Citizenship, March 1933, Chicago Illinois.

11. Ibid.

12. Ibid.

13. James W. Sanders, *The Education of an Urban Minority* (New York: Oxford University Press, 1977), 45.

14. Ibid., 46–47.

15. Note that religious persecution was not listed as a reason for sending children to Catholic schools. By 1875, practices such as reading the King James version of the Bible ended. The Protestant orientation remained in public schools throughout the nineteenth century because the majority of teachers were Protestant until the twentieth century. See Ellen Skerrett, "The Catholic Dimension," in *The Irish in Chicago,* eds. Lawrence J. McCaffrey, Ellen Skerrett, Michael F. Funchion, and Charles Fanning (Urbana: University of Illinois Press, 1987), 44–46.

16. Joseph Shaw, *The Catholic Parish as a Way-Station of Ethnicity and Americanization: Chicago's Germans and Italians* (New York: Carlson, 1991), 120.

17. Lopato, 63.

18. Skerrett, 46.

19. Ibid., 44.

20. Ibid., 45.

21. Ibid.

22. Joseph Parot, "The American Faith and the Persistence of Chicago Polonia, 1870–1920," Ph.D. dissertation, Northern Illinois University, 1984.

23. Ibid.

24. Ibid.

25. Ibid.

26. Lopato, 63.

27. Martha Leszcyk—032, Oral History Archives of Chicago Polonia, Chicago Historical Society, Chicago Illinois.

28. Ibid.

29. Ibid.

30. Shaw, 122.

31. Ibid.

32. Proceedings of the Board of Education of the city of Chicago, 1923.

33. Andrzej Brozek, *Polish Americans 1854–1939* (Warsaw, Poland: Interpress, 1985), 150.

34. Ibid.

35. Shaw, 123.
36. Ibid.
37. Annual Report of the Board of Education of the city of Chicago 1900–1901.
38. Edith Abbott and Sophonisba P. Breckinridge, *Truancy and Non-Attendance in the Chicago Schools* (New York: Arno Press, 1970), 264, 266.
39. Ibid., 286.
40. Annual Report of the Board of Education of the city of Chicago, 1917–1918.
41. Ibid.
42. Margaret Sabella—53, Italian American Oral History Project, University of Illinois, Chicago, Illinois.
43. Annual Report of the Board of Education of the city of Chicago, 1911–1912.
44. Ibid.
45. Chicago Board of Education, Annual Report of the Superintendent of Compulsory Education for the School Year Ending June 29, 1923.
46. Ibid.
47. Ibid.
48. Hilda Satt Polacheck, *I Came a Stranger* (Urbana: University of Illinois Press, 1989), 25–26.
49. Ibid., 26.
50. Counseling Session 7–27, 1950, Scholarship and Guidance Association, University of Illinois, Chicago Illinois.
51. Ibid.
52. Ibid.
53. Ibid.
54. Ibid.
55. Service Council for Girls 1925–1947, United Charities, Chicago Historical Society, Chicago, Illinois.
56. Bodnar, 81.
57. Ibid.
58. Ibid.
59. Ibid.
60. Maria Vallani—80, Italian American Oral History Project, University of Illinois, Chicago, Illinois.
61. Ibid.
62. Edson, 148.
63. Sydelle Kramer and Jenny Masur, eds. *Jewish Grandmothers* (Boston: Beacon Press, 1976), 62, 64.
64. Counseling Session 3–25, 1950, Scholarship and Guidance Association, University of Illinois, Chicago Illinois.
65. Ibid.

66. Ibid.

67. Counseling Session 7–27, 1950, Scholarship and Guidance Association, University of Illinois, Chicago Illinois.

68. Scholarship and Guidance Association Case Studies 6, 74–7, Scholarship and Guidance Association, University of Illinois, Chicago, Illinois.

69. Counseling Session 3–25, 1950, Scholarship and Guidance Association, University of Illinois, Chicago Illinois.

70. Ibid.

71. Ibid.

72. Ibid.

73. Ibid.

74. Ronald Sams, interview by author, Riverdale, Illinois, June 24, 2000.

75. Ibid.

76. Kevin Robinson, interview by author, Riverdale, Illinois, June 24, 2000.

77. Ibid.

78. Ibid.

79. Counseling Session 3–39, 1950, Scholarship and Guidance Association, University of Illinois, Chicago Illinois.

80. Ibid.

81. Ibid.

82. Scholarship and Guidance Association Case Studies 9–42, 74–7, 1957, Scholarship and Guidance Association, University of Illinois, Chicago, Illinois.

83. Ibid.

84. Richard White described his mother's experience in beauty school in a similar manner. However, his interpretation that she was singled out as the "before shot for the ultimate makeover" and a "guinea pig" was not necessarily accurate. Because he did not use a direct quote from his mother in which she described her experiences in her own words, I am not convinced that she was experimented on any more or less than the other students because it is a common practice for beauty school students to practice performing services on each other. See Richard White, *Remembering Ahanagran* (New York: Hill and Wang, 1998), 177–179.

85. Emma Kowalenko, "The Image and Self Image of Chicago Polonia Women, 1915–1945," Master's thesis, Northeastern Illinois University, 1984.

86. Counts, 237–39.

87. Ibid., 241.

88. Ibid., 243.

89. Ibid., 244.

90. Ibid., 245.

91. Finegold, 164; Dick Simpson, *Rogues, Rebels, and Rubber Stamps: The Politics of the Chicago City Council from 1863 to the Present* (Boulder, CO: Westview Press, 2001), 90.
92. Loomis, 22–23.
93. Finegold, 164.
94. Ibid.
95. Margaret Sabella—53.
96. Ibid.
97. Kowalenko, 28–29.
98. David John Hogan, *Class and Reform: School and Society in Chicago, 1880–1890* (Philadelphia: University of Pennsylvania Press, 1985), 198.
99. Ibid.
100. Ibid.
101. Proceedings of the Board of Education of the City of Chicago, 1929.
102. Ibid.
103. Margaret Sabella—53.
104. Scholarship and Guidance Association Report, 74–7, Scholarship and Guidance Association, University of Illinois, Chicago, Illinois.
105. Ibid.
106. Scholarship and Guidance Association Case Studies, 7–27, 74–7, Scholarship and Guidance Association University of Illinois, Chicago, Illinois.
107. Ibid.
108. Ibid.
109. Ibid.
110. *Austin News*, June 1958, Austin High Collection, Harold Washington Library, Chicago Illinois.
111. Ibid.
112. *Chicago Daily Tribune*, April 4, 1900.
113. Ibid.
114. Ibid.
115. 61st Congress, 3rd Session, Reports of the Immigration Commission, *The Children of Immigrants in Schools*, vol. 2 (Metuchen, NJ: Scarecrow Reprint Corporation, 1970), 682.
116. Ibid.
117. Ibid.
118. Skerrett, 45.
119. *The Green and White*, December 3, 1919.
120. *Chicago Tribune*, November 16, 1919.
121. Ibid.
122. Proceedings of the Board of Education of the city of Chicago, 1934.
123. Proceedings of the Board of Education of the city of Chicago, 1932.
124. Proceedings of the Board of Education of the city of Chicago, 1934.
125. *Chicago Tribune*, 9 May, 1934.

126. Dominic Pandolfi—27, Italian American Oral History Project, University of Illinois, Chicago, Illinois.
127. Ibid.
128. Ibid.

Chapter 4

1. Dinnerstein, 44.
2. Ibid., 44–45.
3. Ibid., 45.
4. Ibid.
5. Ibid.
6. Shapiro, 5.
7. Ibid.
8. Govsky, 62.
9. Ibid.
10. Ibid., 64.
11. Sharrow, 81–82.
12. Ibid., 82–83.
13. Tsilia Michlin Goldin, "Not by Bread Alone," in *Line Five: The Internal Passport*, eds. Elaine Pomper Snyderman and Margaret Thomas Witknosky (Chicago: Chicago Review Press, 1992), 5–6.
14. Ibid.
15. Julia Zissman Umanstev, "A Reduction of Remedies," in *Line Five*, 103–106.
16. Ibid.
17. Ibid., 107.
18. Anya Pavel (pseudonym) in *Line Five*, 274.
19. Ibid.
20. Ibid.
21. Jeffrey Brooks, *When Russia Learned to Read: Literacy and Popular Literature, 1861–1917* (Princeton: Princeton University Press, 1985), 245.
22. Baskerville, 82.
23. Ibid., 83.
24. Ibid.
25. Ibid., 82.
26. Cowan and Cowan, 78.
27. Ibid.
28. Ibid.
29. Ibid., 82.
30. Ibid.

31. Baskerville, 88.
32. Cowan and Cowan, 78.
33. Baskerville, 86.
34. Rose Sorkin, "Rose Sorkin," in *Jewish Grandmothers*, 31.
35. Ibid., 33.
36. Ibid.
37. Ibid., 33–34.
38. Francesco Cordasco, "The Children of Immigrants in the Schools: Historical Analogues of Educational Deprivation," *The Journal of Negro Education* 42 (1973): 45–46.
39. Dinnerstein, 45.
40. Dinnerstein, 45–46.
41. Ibid., 47.
42. Ibid., 46.
43. Bodnar, 81.
44. Abbott and Breckinridge, 128–147.
45. Annual Meeting Reports for the Years 1920–1924, Scholarship Guidance and Association, Chicago, Illinois, UIC Special Collections.
46. Abbott and Breckinridge.
47. Ibid.
48. Ibid.
49. Annual Meeting Reports for the Years 1920–1924; Vocational Supervision League Report of Scholarship Work, September 1920–June 1921, Scholarship and Guidance Association, UIC Special Collections.
50. Service Reports, Scholarship and Guidance Association, UIC Special Collections.
51. Vocational Supervision League Annual Report, 1926, Scholarship and Guidance Association, UIC Special Collections; Service Reports, 1912–1964, Scholarship and Guidance Association, UIC Special Collections.
52. Shapiro, 10.
53. Ibid., 11.
54. Cowan and Cowan, 92.
55. Counseling Session 7–27, 1950, Scholarship and Guidance Association, UIC Special Collections.
56. Psychiatric and Physical Report 1–4, 12 August 1958, Scholarship and Guidance Association, UIC Special Collections.
57. Ibid.
58. Ibid.
59. Linker, 94.
60. Intake Report 3–25, 1957, Scholarship and Guidance Association, UIC Special Collections.
61. Edson, 147–148.
62. Ibid.

63. Social Worker's Report to SGA 1–3, May 1, 1958, Scholarship and Guidance Association, UIC Special Collections.

64. Salvatore LaGumina, "American Education and the Italian Immigrant Response," in *American Education and the European Immigrant*, ed. Bernard J. Weiss (Urbana: University of Illinois, 1982), 63.

65. Ibid.

66. Ibid.

67. Elena Teruty—9, Italian American Oral History Project, UIC Special Collections.

68. Edson, 257.

69. Edson's dissertation on immigrant schooling between 1880 and 1920 contained few specific dates. Most of the accounts that he used in his thesis did not have dates listed.

70. Ibid., 239.

71. Ibid.

72. Ibid., 367–68.

73. Covello, 252–53.

74. Edson, 223.

75. Ibid.

76. Ibid., 236.

77. Ibid., 238.

78. Ibid.

79. Marietta Interlandi—15, Italian Oral History Project, UIC Special Collections.

80. Edson, 196, 231.

81. Ibid., 231.

82. Ibid., 237.

83. Rosamond Mirabella—69, Italian Oral History Project, UIC Special Collections.

84. Joachim Martorano—91, Italian Immigrant History Project, UIC Special Collections.

85. Mary Argenzio—90, Italian Immigrant History Project, UIC Special Collections.

86. Ibid.

87. Ibid.

88. Martorano—91, Italian Immigrant History Project, UIC Special Collections.

89. Ibid.

90. Lina Tarabori—79, Italian American Oral History Project, UIC Special Collections.

91. Mary Manella—51, Italian American Oral History Project, UIC Special Collections.

92. Covello, 292.

93. Ibid, 295.

94. Lina Tarabori—79, Italian American Oral History Project, UIC Special Collections.

95. Therese Giannetti—55, Italian American Oral History Project, UIC Special Collections.

96. Dante A. Greco—67, Italian American Oral History Project, UIC Special Collections.

97. Sam Ori—57, Italian American Oral History Project, UIC Special Collections.

98. Florence Roselli—44, Italian American Oral History Project, UIC Special Collections.

99. Ibid.

100. Ibid.

101. Rose Clementi—47, Italian American Oral History Project, UIC Special Collections.

102. Ibid.

103. Ibid.

104. Case 2–40, Scholarship and Guidance Association, 1957, UIC Special Collections.

105. Edson, 320.

106. Dominic Pandolfi—28, Italian American Oral History Project, UIC Special Collections.

107. Edson, 398.

108. Murray, 113.

109. Ibid.; Martha Leszcyk—032, Oral History Archives of Chicago Polonia, CHS Manuscripts and Archives.

110. Murray, 113.

111. Ibid.

112. Ibid.

113. Ibid., 209.

114. Ibid.

115. Ibid.

116. Victoria Majerski—088, Oral History Archives of Chicago Polonia, CHS Manuscripts and Archives.

117. Ibid.

118. Ibid.

119. Martha Leszcyk—032, Oral History Archives of Chicago Polonia, CHS Manuscripts and Archives.

120. William Thomas and Florian Znaniecki, *The Polish Peasant in Europe and America* (Urbana: University of Illinois Press, 1984), 21.

121. John Rury, *Education and Women's Work* (Albany: State University of New York, 1991), 135.

122. Ibid., 139.

123. Ibid.
124. Bodnar, 82.
125. Ibid.
126. Ibid.
127. Ibid.
128. Ibid.
129. Interview, 3 November 1933, United Charities, CHS Manuscripts and Archives.
130. Ibid.
131. Kowalenko, 106–108.
132. Bodnar, 81.
133. Ibid.
134. Ibid.
135. Leszcyk.
136. Mary Janka—116, Oral History Archives of Chicago Polonia, CHS Manuscripts and Archives.
137. Virginia Martell—106, Oral History Archives of Chicago Polonia, CHS Manuscripts and Archives.
138. Ibid.
139. Ibid.
140. Social Worker's Report (1–40), 13 February 1953, Scholarship and Guidance Association.
141. Ibid.
142. Bodnar, 82.
143. Walter Bronwen, *Outsiders Inside: Whiteness, Place, and Irish Women* (New York: Routledge, 2001), 16.
144. Luddy, 90.
145. Ibid.
146. Ibid.
147. Ibid.
148. MacCurtain and O'Corrain, 47.
149. Ibid.
150. Ibid.
151. Ibid.
152. Fitzpatrick, 234.
153. Ibid., 235.
154. Ibid.
155. Luddy, 146.
156. Beale, 130.
157. Ibid.
158. O'Carroll, 74.
159. Ibid., 65.
160. Ibid.
161. Ibid., 71.

162. Ibid., 72–73.

163. Ibid., 74.

164. Ibid.

165. Beale, 127.

166. Andrew M. Greeley, *The Irish Americans: The Rise to Money and Power* (New York: Harper and Row, 1981), 114.

167. Ibid., 72.

168. Ibid., 73.

169. Ibid., 2.

170. Ibid., 114.

171. Ibid., 2.

172. Ibid., 122.

173. Robert L. Reid, ed., *Battleground: The Autobiography of Margaret A. Haley* (Urbana: University of Illinois Press, 1982), ix.

174. Ibid.

175. Skerrett, 35.

176. Hasia R. Diner, *Erin's Daughters in America* (Baltimore: Johns Hopkins University Press, 1983), 133.

177. McCaffrey, 8–9.

178. Ibid.

179. Mary C. Donelin, "American Irish Women Firsts," *Journal of the American Irish Historical Society* 24 (1925): 216.

180. Ibid.

181. Ibid., 217.

182. Ibid., 218.

183. Ibid., 215.

184. McCaffrey, 16.

185. Ibid.

186. Ibid.

187. Greeley, 119.

Bibliography

Books and Book Chapters

Abbott, Edith, and Sophonisba Breckinridge. *Truancy and Non-Attendance in the Chicago Schools.* New York: Arno Press, 1970.

Addams, Jane. "The Public School and the Immigrant Child, 1908." In *Jane Addams on Education,* ed. Ellen Cordliffe Lagemann, 136–142. New York: Teachers College Press, 1985.

———. *The Second Twenty Years at Hull House September 1909 to September 1929.* New York: Macmillan, 1930.

Angus, David L., and Jeffrey E. Mirel. *The Failed Promise of the American High School 1890–1995.* New York: Teachers College Press, 1999.

Appel, John, and Selma Appel. "The Huddled Masses and the Little Red Schoolhouse." In *American Education and the European Immigrant: 1840–1940,* ed. Bernard Weiss, 17–30. Urbana: University of Illinois Press, 1982.

Baldwin, James. "On Being 'White' and Other Lies." In *Black on White: Writers on What It Means to Be White,* ed. David Roediger, 177–180. New York: Schocken Books, 1998.

Barret, James R., and David Roediger. "How White People Became White." In *Critical White Studies: Looking Behind the Mirror,* ed. Richard Delgado and Jean Stefancic, 402–406. Philadelphia: Temple University Press, 1997.

———. "Inbetween Peoples: Race, Nationality, and the New Immigrant Working Class." In *Majority and Minority: The Dynamics of Race and Ethnicity in American Life,* ed. Norman R. Yetman, 144–159. Boston: Allyn and Bacon, 1999.

Baskerville, Beatrice C. *The Polish Jew.* London: Chapman and Hall, 1906.

Beale, Jenny. *Women in Ireland*. Bloomington: Indiana University Press, 1987.

Berg, Barbara J. *The Remembered Gate: Origins of American Feminism; The Woman and the City, 1800–1860*. New York: Oxford University Press, 1978.

Bernstein, Abraham. *The Education of Urban Populations*. New York: Random House, 1967.

Berrol, Selma Cantor. *Growing Up American: Immigrant Children. Then and Now*. New York: Twayne Publishers, 1995.

———. "Public Schools and Immigrants: The New York City Experience." In *American Education and the European Immigrant: 1840–1940*, ed. Bernard Weiss, 31–43. Urbana: University of Illinois Press, 1982.

Bierstadt, Edward H. *Aspects of Americanization*. Cincinnati: National Americanization Committee, 1922.

Bodnar, John. "Schooling and the Slavic-American Family, 1900–1940." In *American Education and the European Immigrant: 1840–1940*, ed. Bernard Weiss, 78–95. Urbana: University of Illinois Press, 1982.

Bogen, Elisabeth. *Immigration in New York*. New York: Praeger Publishers, 1987.

Bolek, Francis. *The Polish American School System*. New York: Columbia Press Corp., 1948.

Booth, Alan, Ann C. Crouter, and Nancy Lardale. *Immigration and the Family: Research and Policy on U.S. Immigrants*. Hillsdale, NJ: Lawrence Erlbaum Associates, 1997.

Brickman, William W. *Bibliographical Essays on the History and Philosophy of Education*. Norwood, PA: Norwood Editions, 1975.

Bronwen, Walter. *Outsiders Inside: Whiteness, Place, and Irish Women*. New York: Routledge, 2001.

Brooks, Jeffrey. *When Russia Learned to Read*. Princeton: Princeton University Press, 1985.

Brozek, Andrzej. *Polish Americans, 1854–1939*. Warsaw, Poland: Interpress, 1985.

Brumberg, Stephan F. *Going to America, Going to School: The Jewish Immigrant Public School Encounter in Turn-of-the-Century New York City*. New York: Praeger Publishers, 1986.

Byrne, Anne and Madeline Leonard, eds. *Women and Irish Society*. Belfast: Beyond the Pale Publications, 1997.

Bryne, Stephen. *Irish Emigration to the United States*. New York: Arno Press and *The New York Times*, 1969.

Calvo, Janet M. "Spouse-Based Immigration Laws: The Legacy of Coverture." In *Critical Race Feminism*, ed. Adrien Katherine Wing, 380–386. New York: New York University Press, 1997.

Chicago Board of Education. *Historical Sketches of the Public School System of the City of Chicago, to the Close of the School Year 1880.* Chicago: Clark & Edwards Printers, 1880.

Clark, Charles. *Uprooting Otherness.* Selingsgrove, PA: Susquehanna University Press, 2000.

Clark, Dennis. *Hibernia America: The Irish and Regional Cultures.* New York: Greenwood Press, 1986.

Cohen, Sol. *Education in the United States: A Documentary History.* New York: Random House, 1973.

Conant, James Bryant. *Slums and Suburbs: A Commentary on Schools in Metropolitan Areas.* New York: McGraw-Hill Book Company, 1961.

Cott, Nancy F. *The Bonds of Womanhood: "Woman's Sphere" in New England, 1780–1835.* New Haven: Yale University Press, 1977.

Counts, George S. *School and Society in Chicago.* New York: Arno Press, 1971.

Covello, Francesco. *Immigrant Children in American Schools.* Fairfield, NJ: Augustus M. Kelley, 1976.

Covello, Leonard. *The Social Background of the Italo-American School Child.* New York: Rowman and Littlefield, 1972.

Cremin, Lawrence Arthur. *American Education, the Metropolitan Experience 1876–1980.* New York: Harper & Row, 1988.

———. *Popular Education and Its Discontents.* New York: Oxford University Press, 1989.

———. *The Transformation of the School.* New York: Alfred A. Knopf, 1968.

Cubberly, Ellwood P. *Public Education in the United States,* 2nd ed., rev. Boston: Houghton Mifflin, 1934.

Cutler, Irving. *The Jews of Chicago: From Shetetl to Suburb.* Urbana: University of Illinois Press, 1996.

Dentler, Robert A., and Anne L. Hafner. *Hosting Newcomers and Structuring Educational Opportunities for Immigrant Children.* New York: Teachers College Press, 1997.

Diner, Hasia R. *Erin's Daughters in America.* Baltimore: Johns Hopkins University Press, 1983.

Dinnerstein, Leonard. "Education and the Advancement of American Jews." In *American Education and the European Immigrant: 1840–1940,* ed. Bernard J. Weiss, 44–60. Urbana: University of Illinois Press, 1982.

Diver-Stamnes, Ann C. *Lives in the Balance: Youth, Poverty, and Education in Watts.* Albany: State University of New York Press, 1995.

Dodge, Chester C. *Reminiscences of a School Master.* Chicago: Ralph Fletcher Seymour, 1941.

Duncan, Hannibal C. *Immigration and Assimilation.* Boston: D.C. Heath, 1933.

Eklof, Ben. "Schooling and Literacy in Late Imperial Russia." In *Literacy in Historical Perspective*, ed. Daniel P. Resnick, 105–128. Washington, D.C.: Library of Congress, 1983.

Fass, Paula A. *Outside in: Minorities and the Transformation of American Education*. New York: Oxford University Press, 1989.

Feinberg, Walter, Harvey Kantor, Michael Katz, and Paul Violas. *Revisionists Respond to Ravitch*. Washington, D.C.: National Academy of Education, 1980.

Finegold, Kenneth. *Experts and Politicians: Reform Challenges to Machine Politics in New York, Cleveland, and Chicago*. Princeton: Princeton University Press, 1995.

Fitzpatrick, David. *The Two Irelands: 1912–1939*. Oxford: Oxford University Press, 1998.

Flanagan, Maureen Anne. *Charter Reform in Chicago, 1890–1915*. Carbondale: Southern Illinois University Press, 1989.

Fox, Paul. *The Poles in America*. New York: Arno Press, 1970.

Frankenburg, Ruth. "White Women, Race Matters: The Social Construction of Whiteness." In *Critical White Studies: Looking Behind the Mirror*, ed. Richard Delgado and Jean Stefancic, 629–631. Philadelphia: Temple University Press, 1997.

Franklin, Vincent P. *The Education of Black Philadelphia: The Social History of a Minority Community, 1900–1950*. Philadelphia: University of Pennsylvania Press, 1979.

Gallman, J. Matthew. *Receiving Erin's Children*. Chapel Hill: University of North Carolina Press, 2000.

Gittell, Marilyn, ed. *Educating an Urban Population*. Beverly Hills, CA: Sage Publications, 1967.

Glazer, Nathan. "Immigrants and Education." In *Clamor at the Gates: The New American Immigration*, ed. Nathan Glazer, 213–39. San Francisco: Institute for Contemporary Studies, 1985.

Gordon, Ann D., Mari Jo Buhle, and Nancy Schrom Dye. "The Problem of Women's History." In *Liberating Women's History: Theoretical and Critical Essays*, ed. Berenice A. Carroll, 75–92. Urbana: University of Illinois Press, 1976.

Gordon, Milton M. "Assimilation in America: Theory and Reality." In *Majority and Minority: The Dynamics of Race and Ethnicity in American Life*, ed. Norman R. Yetman, 272–84. Boston: Allyn and Bacon, 1999.

Grace, Gerald. *Education and the City: Theory, History, and Contemporary Practice*. London: Routledge & Kegan Paul, 1984.

Greeley, Andrew. *That Most Distressful Nation: The Taming of the American Irish*. Chicago: Quadrangle Books, 1972.

———. *The Irish Americans: The Rise to Money and Power*. New York: Harper and Row, 1981.

Greer, Colin. *The Great School Legend: A Revisionist Interpretation of American Public Education.* New York: Viking, 1973.

Grillo, Trina, and Stephanie M. Wildman. "Obscuring the Importance of Race: The Implication of Making Comparisons between Racism and Sexism (or other isms)." In *Critical Race Feminism,* ed. Adrien Katherine Wing, 44–50. New York: New York University Press, 1997.

Grossman, Herbert. *Land of Hope: Chicago Black Southerners, and the Great Migration.* Chicago: University of Illinois Press, 1989.

Hagen, William W. *Germans, Poles, and Jews.* Chicago: University of Chicago Press, 1980.

Handlin, Oscar. "Education and the European Immigrant 1820–1920." In *American Education and the European Immigrant: 1840–1940,* ed. Bernard Weiss, 3–16. Urbana: University of Illinois Press, 1982.

Harris, Angela P. "Race and Essentialism in Feminist Legal Theory." In *Critical Race Feminism,* ed. Adrien Katherine Wing, 11–18. New York: New York University Press, 1997.

Hartmann, Edward. *The Americanization of the Immigrant.* New York: Columbia University Press, 1948.

Havighurst, Robert J. *Education in Metropolitan Areas.* Boston: Allyn and Bacon, 1966.

Herscher, Uri D., ed. *The East European Jewish Experience in America.* Cincinnati: American Jewish Archives, 1983.

Hirabayashi, Lane Ryo. *Teaching Asian American: Diversity & the Problem of Community.* New York: Rowan & Littlefield, 1998.

Hogan, David John. *Class and Reform: School and Society in Chicago, 1880–1890.* Philadelphia: University of Pennsylvania Press, 1985.

Hones, David F. *Educating New Americans: Immigrant Lives and Learning.* Mahwah, NJ: Lawrence Erlbaum Associates, 1999.

Howatt, John. *Notes on the First One-Hundred Years of Chicago School History.* Chicago: Washburne Trade Press, 1940.

Hsia, Jayjia, *Asian Americans in Higher Education and at Work.* Hillsdale, NJ: Lawrence Erlbaum Associates, 1988.

Igoa, Christine. *The Inner World of the Immigrant Child.* Hillsdale, NJ: Lawrence Erlbaum Associates, 1995.

Ireland, Tom. *Ireland: Past and Present.* New York: G. P. Putnam's Sons, 1942.

Kaestle, Carl. *The Evolution of an Urban School System: New York City, 1750–1850.* Cambridge: Harvard University Press, 1973.

Kantor, Harvey, and David B. Tyack, eds. *Work, Youth, and Schooling: Historical Perspectives on Vocationalism in American Education.* Stanford: Stanford University Press, 1982.

Karier, Clarence J., Paul Violas, and Joel Spring. *Roots of Crisis: American Education in the Twentieth Century.* Chicago: Rand McNally, 1973.

Karp, Abraham. *Golden Door to America: The Jewish Immigrant Experience.* New York: Viking Press, 1976.

Katz, Michael B. *Improving Poor People: The Welfare State, The "Underclass," and Urban Schools as History.* Princeton: Princeton University Press, 1995.

———. *School Reform: Past and Present.* Boston: Little Brown and Company, 1971.

———. *The Irony of Early School Reform: Educational Innovation in Mid-Nineteenth-Century Massachusetts.* Cambridge: Harvard University Press, 1968.

Kazal, Russell A. "Revisiting Assimilation: The Rise, Fall, and Reappraisal of a Concept in American Ethnic History." In *Majority and Minority: The Dynamics of Race and Ethnicity in American Life,* ed. Norman R. Yetman, 285–311. Boston: Allyn and Bacon, 1999.

Kerber, August, and Barbara Bommarito, eds. *The Schools and the Urban Crisis.* New York: Holt, Rinehart, Winston, 1965.

Kessner, Thomas. *The Golden Door: Italian and Jewish Immigrant Mobility in New York City: 1880–1915.* New York: Oxford University Press, 1977.

Knoll, Ignatoff. *How the Irish Became White.* New York: Routledge, 1995.

Kopan, Andrew T. *Education and Greek Immigrants in Chicago, 1892–1973: A Study in Ethnic Survival.* New York: Garland Publications, 1990.

Krug, Edward A. *The Shaping of the American High School, 1920–1941.* Madison: University of Wisconsin Press, 1972.

LaGumina, Salvatore. "American Education and the Italian Immigrant Response." In *American Education and the European Immigrant: 1840–1940,* ed. Bernard Weiss, 61–77. Urbana: University of Illinois Press, 1982.

Langelan, Martha. *Back Off! How to Confront and Stop Sexual Harassment and Harassers.* New York: Fireside, 1993.

Lazerson, Marvin. *Origins of the Urban School: Public Education in Massachusetts, 1870–1915.* Cambridge: Harvard University Press, 1971.

Lee, Joseph J. "Women and the Church Since the Famine." In *Women in Irish Society: The Historical Dimension,* ed. Margaret MacCurtain and Donneha O'Corrain, 37–45. Westport, CT: Greenwood Press, 1979.

Lopato, Helena Znaniecka. *Polish Americans.* New Brunswick, NJ: Transaction Publishers, 1994.

Luddy, Maria. *Women in Ireland, 1800–1918.* Cork, Ireland: Cork University Press, 1995.

MacCurtain, Margaret, and Donneha O'Corrain, eds. *Women in Irish Society: The Historical Dimension.* Westport, CT: Greenwood Press, 1979.

MacKinnon, Catherine A. "From Practice and Theory, or What Is a White Woman Anyway?" In *Critical White Studies: Looking Behind the Mirror,* ed. Richard Delgado and Jean Stefancic, 300–304. Philadelphia: Temple University Press, 1997.

Maguire, John Francis. *The Irish in America*. New York: Arno Press and the *New York Times*, 1969.

Mahoney, Martha R. "Racial Construction and Woman as Differentiated Actors." In *Critical White Studies: Looking Behind the Mirror*, ed. Richard Delgado and Jean Stefancic, 305–309. Philadelphia: Temple University Press, 1997.

McCaffrey, Lawrence J. "The Irish-American Dimension." In *The Irish in Chicago*, ed. Lawrence J. McCaffrey, Ellen Skerrett, Michael F. Funchion, and Charles Fanning, 1–21. Urbana: University of Illinois Press, 1987.

———. "Conclusion." In *The Irish in Chicago*, ed. Lawrence J. McCaffrey, Ellen Skerrett, Michael F. Funchion, and Charles Fanning, 146–158. Urbana: University of Illinois Press, 1987.

McDonnell, Lorraine M., and Paul T. Hill. *New Comers in American Schools: Meeting the Educational Needs of Immigrant Youth*. Santa Monica, CA: RAND, 1993.

McIntosh, Peggy. "White Privilege and Male Privilege: A Personal Account of Coming to See Correspondences through Work in Women's Studies." In *Critical White Studies: Looking Behind the Mirror*, ed. Richard Delgado and Jean Stefancic, 291–299. Philadelphia: Temple University Press, 1997.

McLemore, William Prince. *Foundations of Urban Education*. Washington, D.C.: University Press of America, 1977.

McMahon, Eileen. *What Parish Are You From? A Chicago Irish Community and Race Relations*. Lexington: University of Kentucky, 1995.

Meites, Hyman L., ed. *History of the Jews of Chicago*. Facsimile of the original 1924 edition. Chicago: Chicago Jewish Historical Society and Wellington Publishing, 1990.

Miller, Harry L. *Social Foundations of Education: Urban Focus*. New York: Holt, Rinehart, and Winston, 1970.

Miller, Harry L., and Marjorie B. Smiley. *Education in the Metropolis*. New York: Free Press, 1967.

Miller, Kerby A. *Emigrants and Exiles*. New York: Oxford University Press, 1985.

———. *Irish Popular Culture, 1650–1850*. Ballsbridge, Ireland: Irish Academic Press, 1999.

Mirel, Jeffrey. *The Rise and Fall of an Urban School System: Detroit, 1907–1981*. Ann Arbor: University of Michigan Press, 1993.

Moreo, Dominic W. *Schools in the Great Depression*. New York: Garland Publishing, 1996.

Murray, Michael. *Poland's Progress 1919–1931*. London: Orbis, 1945.

Nathan, Maud. *The Story of an Epoch-Making Movement*. New York: Doubleday, 1926.

National Coalition of Advocates for Students. *New Voices: Immigrant Students in U.S. Public Schools*. Boston: National Coalition of Advocates for Students, 1988.

Nelli, Humbert S. *From Immigrants to Ethnics: Italian Americans.* New York: Oxford University Press, 1983.

O'Carroll, Ide. *Models for Movers: Irish Women's Emigration to America.* Dublin: Attic Press, 1990.

Olneck, Michael R. "Immigrants and Education." In *Handbook of Multicultural Education,* ed. James A. Banks and Cherry A. McGee Banks, 310–327. New York: Simon & Schuster, 1995.

Olsen, Laurie. *Made in America: Immigrant Students in Our Public Schools.* New York: W.W. Norton, 1997.

O'Sullivan, Patrick, ed. *Irish Women and Irish Migration.* London: Leicester University Press, 1995.

Pacyga, Dominic A. *Polish Immigrants and Industrial Chicago: Workers on the South Side, 1880–1922.* Columbus: Ohio State University Press, 1991.

Park, Clara C., and Marilyn Mei-Ying Chi. *Asian-American Education: Prospects and Challenges.* Westport, CT: Bergin & Garvey, 1999.

Parker, Franklin, and Betty June Parker. *Women's Education—A World View.* Westport, CT: Greenwood Press, 1979.

Payne, Charles. *Getting What We Ask For: The Ambiguity of Success and Failure in Urban Education.* Westport, CT: Greenwood Press, 1984.

Perlmann, Joel. *Ethnic Differences: Schooling and Social Structure among the Irish, Italians, Jews, and Blacks in an American City, 1880–1935.* New York: Cambridge University Press, 1988.

———. *Literacy among the Jews of Russia in 1897: A Reanalysis of Census Data.* New York: Jerome Levy Economics Institute, 1996.

Ravitch, Diane. *The Revisionist Revised.* New York: Basic Books, 1978.

Reese, William J. *Power and the Promise of School Reform: Grassroots Movements during the Progressive Era.* Boston: Routledge & Kegan Paul, 1986.

Roberts, Peter. *The New Immigration: A Study of the Industrial and Social Life of Southeastern Europeans in America.* New York: Arno Press and the *New York Times,* 1970.

Rolle, Andrew. *The Italian Americans: Troubled Roots.* New York: Free Press, 1980.

Rosaldo, Michelle Zimbalist, and Louise Lamphere, eds. *Woman, Culture, and Society.* Stanford: Stanford University Press, 1974.

Rozin, Anna. *Mightier Than the Sword: An Analysis of the Promotion of Literacy in Nineteenth-Century Pre-emancipation Russia.* Ann Arbor: University of Michigan, 1995.

Rury, John. *Education and Women's Work.* New York: State University of New York, 1991.

Sacks, Karen Brodkin. "How Did Jews Become White Folks?" In *Critical White Studies: Looking Behind the Mirror,* ed. Richard Delgado and Jean Stefancic, 395–401. Philadelphia: Temple University Press, 1997.

Sanders, James W. *The Education of an Urban Minority.* New York: Oxford University Press, 1977.

Schiavo, Giovanni Ermenegildo. *The Italians in Chicago: A Study in Americanization.* New York: Arno Press, 1975.

Shah, Sonia. *Dragon Ladies: American Feminists Breathe Fire.* Boston: South End Press, 1997.

Shaw, Joseph. *The Catholic Parish as a Way-Station of Ethnicity and Americanization: Chicago's Germans and Italians.* New York: Carlson, 1991.

Skerrett, Ellen. "The Catholic Dimension." In *The Irish in Chicago,* ed. Lawrence J. McCaffrey, Ellen Skerrett, Michael F. Funchion, and Charles Fanning, 22–60. Urbana: University of Illinois Press, 1987.

Steinberg, Stephen. *The Ethnic Myth: Race, Ethnicity, and Class in America.* Boston: Beacon, 1989.

Stewart, David W. *Immigration and Education: The Crisis of Opportunities.* New York: Lexington Books, 1993.

Stromquist, Nelly P., ed. *Education in Urban Areas: Cross-National Dimensions.* Westport, CT: Praeger, 1994.

Thomas, William I., and Florian Znaniecki, *The Polish Peasant in Europe and America.* Urbana: University of Illinois Press, 1984.

Townshend, Charles. *Ireland: The Twentieth Century.* London: Arnold, 1998.

Troen, Selwyn K. *The Public and the Schools: Shaping the St. Louis System, 1838–1920.* Columbia: University of Missouri Press, 1975.

Tyack, David. "New Perspectives on the History of American Education." In *The State of American History,* ed. Herbert J. Bass. Chicago: Quadrangle Books, 1970.

———. *The One Best System: A History of American Urban Education.* Cambridge: Harvard University Press, 1974.

Tyack, David, and Elisabeth Hansot. *Learning Together: A History of Coeducation in American Public Schools.* New Haven: Yale University Press, 1990.

Violas, Paul. "Jane Addams and the New Liberalism." In *Roots of Crisis: American Education in the Twentieth Century,* eds. Clarence Karier, Paul Violas, and Joel Spring, 66–83. Chicago: Rand McNally, 1973.

———. *The Training of the Urban Working Class: History of Twentieth Century American Education.* Chicago: Rand McNally, 1978.

Weiss, Bernard J., ed. *American Education and the European Immigrant.* Urbana: University of Illinois Press, 1982.

Weis, Lois. *Class, Race, and Gender in American Education.* Albany: State University of New York Press, 1988.

Weisz, Howard. *Irish-American and Italian-American Educational Views, 1870–1900: A Comparison.* New York: Arno Press, 1976.

Wrigley, Julia. *Class, Politics, and Public Schools: Chicago, 1900–1950.* New Brunswick, NJ: Rutgers University Press, 1982.

Yamate, Sandra. "Chapter 4: Asian Pacific American Children's Literature: Expanding Perceptions about Who Americans Are." In *Using Multiethnic Literature in the K–8 Classroom,* ed. Violet J. Harris, 95–126. Norwood, MA: Christopher-Gordon Publishers, 1997.

Articles

Atzmon, Ezri. "The Educational Program for Immigrants in the United States." *History of Education Journal* 9 (1958): 75–80.

Aversa, Alfred Jr. "Italian Neo-Ethnicity: The Search for Self-Identity." *Journal of Ethnic Studies* (1978): 49–56.

Band, David. "The New Whiz Kids: Why Asian Americans Are Doing So Well, and What It Costs Them." *Time* (August 1987): 42–51.

Banks, James, and Geneva Gay. *Ethnicity in Contemporary American Society: Toward the Development of a Typology.* (1975) ERIC, ED 121 641.

Carlson, Robert A. "Americanization as an Early Twentieth-Century Adult Education Movement." *History of Education Quarterly* 10 (1970): 440–464.

Clifford, Geraldine Joncich. "History as Experience: The Use of Personal-History Documents in the History of Education." *History of Education* 7 (1978): 183–196.

Cohen, David K. "Immigrants and the Schools." *Review of Educational Research* 40 (1970): 13–27.

Cohen, Miriam. "Changing Educational Strategies Among Immigrant Generations: New York Italians in Comparative Perspectives." *Journal of Social History* 15 (1982): 443–466.

Conway, Jill K. "Perspectives on the History of Women's Education in the United States." *History of Education Quarterly* 14 (1974): 1–12.

Cordasco, Francesco. "The Children of Immigrants in the Schools: Historical Analogues of Educational Deprivation." *The Journal of Negro Education* 42 (1973): 44–54.

Do, Hien Duc. "Two Models from Vietnam." *NEA Today* 16 (1997): 15–19.

Donato, Ruben, and Marvin Lazerson. "New Directions in American Educational History: Problems and Prospects." *Educational Researcher* 29 (2000): 4–15.

Donelin, Mary C. "American Irish Women Firsts." *Journal of the American Irish Historical Society* 24 (1925): 215–221.

Foner, Nancy. "Immigrant Women and Work in New York City, Then and Now." *Journal of American Ethnic History* 18 (1999): 95–107.

Fuchs, Lawrence H. "Immigration, Multiculturalism, and American History." *National Forum* 74 (1994): 42–48.

Galenson, David W. "Neighborhood Effects on the School Attendance of Irish Immigrants' Sons in Boston and Chicago, 1860." *American Journal of Education* 105 (1997): 261–293.

Glenn, Charles L. "Educating the Children of Immigrants." *Phi Delta Kappa* 73 (1992): 404–408.

Holman, Linda Jean. "Meeting the Needs of Hispanic Immigrants." *Educational Leadership* 54 (1997): 37–43.

Huerta-Macias, Ana. "Mi Casa Es Su Casa." *Educational Leadership* 55 (1997): 52–58.

Hunt, Thomas C. "The Schooling of Immigrants and Black Americans: Some Similarities and Differences." *Journal of Negro Education* 45 (1976): 423–431.

Jaret, Charles. "Troubled by Newcomers: Anti-immigrant Attitudes and Action During Two Mass Migrations to the United States." *Journal of American Ethnic History* 18 (1999): 9–11.

Kellor, Frances A. "Education of the Immigrant." *Review* 43 (1914): 21–36.

Kennedy, David M. "Can We Still Afford to Be a Nation of Immigrants?" *The Atlantic Monthly* 278 (1996): 52–63.

Lee, Erika. "Response." *Journal of American Ethnic History* 18 (1999): 157–162.

McIntosh, Peggy. "White Privelege: Unpacking the Invisible Knapsack." *Independent School* (Winter 1990): 31–36.

Montero-Sieburth, Martha, and Mark LaCelle-Peterson. "Immigration and Schooling: An Ethohistorical Account of Policy and Family Perspectives in an Urban Community." *Anthropology and Education Quarterly* 22 (1991): 300–325.

Olneck, Michael R., and Marvin F. Lazerson. "The School Achievement of Immigrant Children: 1900–1930." *History of Education Quarterly* 14 (1974): 453–82.

Olsen, Laurie. "Crossing the Schoolhouse Border: Immigrant Children in California." *Phi Delta Kappa* 70 (1988): 211–218.

O'Meara, John Baptiste. "The Mission of the Irish Race in the United States." *Journal of the American Irish Historical Society* 10 (1911): 105–08.

Portes, Alejandro, and Dag MacLeod. "Educational Progress of Children of Immigrants: The Roles of Class, Ethnicity, and School Context." *Sociology of Education* 69 (1996): 255–275.

Praszalowicz, Dorota. "The Cultural Changes of Polish-American Parochial Schools in Milwaukee, 1866–1988." *Journal of American Ethnic History* 13 (1994): 23–45.

Sicherman, Barbara. "Review Essay: American History." *Signs* 1 (1975): 461–85.

Smith, John, Esq. "The Irishman Ethnologically Considered." *Journal of the American Irish Historical Society* 1 (1898): 51–54.

Smith, Timothy L. "Immigrant Social Aspirations and American Education, 1880–1930." *American Quarterly* 21 (1969): 523–543.

Smith-Rosenberg, Carroll. "The Female World of Love and Ritual: Relations Between Women in Nineteenth-Century America." *Signs* 1 (1975): 1–30.

Tamura, Eileen H. "Gender, Schooling and Teaching, and the Nisei in Hawaii: An Episode in American Immigration History, 1900–1940." *Journal of American Ethnic History* 14 (1995): 3–27.

Thomas, William B. "Urban Schooling for Black Migrant Youth—A Historical Perspective, 1915–1925." *Urban Education* 14 (1979): 267–84.

Tropea, Joseph L. "Bureaucratic Order and Special Children: Urban Schools, 1890s–1940." *History of Education Quarterly* 27 (1987): 29–53.

———. "Bureaucratic Order and Special Children: Urban Schools, 1950s–1960s." *History of Education Quarterly* 27(1987): 339–61.

Ueda, Reed. "Second-Generation Civic America: Education, Citizenship, and the Children of Immigrants." *The Journal of Interdisciplinary History* 29 (1999): 661–676.

Young, Pauline V. "Social Problems in the Education of the Immigrant Child." *American Sociological Review* 1 (1936): 419–429.

Autobiographies and Biographies

Antin, Mary. "The Promised Land," In *Writing Our Lives: Autobiographies of American Jews, 1890–1990*, ed. Steven J. Rubin, 3–19. Philadelphia: The Jewish Publication Society, 1991.

Birmingham, Stephen. *Real Lace: America's Irish Rich*. New York: Harper and Row, 1973.

Chow, Claire S., ed. *Leaving Deep Water: The Lives of Asian American Women at the Crossroads of Two Cultures*. New York: Dutton, 1998.

Cohen, Rosa. *Out of the Shadow*. New York: George Dovan, 1918.

Cowan, Neil M., and Ruth Schwartz Cowan. *Our Parents' Lives*. New Brunswick, NJ: Rutgers University Press, 1989.

Feely, Ida R. "Growing Up on the East Side." In *The East European Jewish Experience in America*, ed. Uri D. Herscher, 113–124. Cincinnati: American Jewish Archives, 1983.

Ffrench, Charles, ed. *Biographical History of the American Irish in Chicago*. Chicago: American Biographical Publishing Co., 1899.

Gmelch, Sharon. *Nan: The Life of an Irish Traveling Woman*. New York: W.W. Norton, 1986.

Goldin, Tsilia Michlin. "Not by Bread Alone." In *Line Five: The Internal Passport*, ed. Elaine Pomper Snyderman and Margaret Thomas Witknosky, 3–10. Chicago: Chicago Review Press, 1992.

Herscher, Uri D., ed. *The East European Jewish Experience in America*. Cincinnati: American Jewish Archives, 1983.

Hibbard, Lydia Beckman. *Reminiscences of Lydia Beckman Hibbard*. Chicago: Privately printed, 1929.

Klotz, Roy. *The Reminiscences of an Adopted Girl in a German Immigrant Community of Chicago*. Pembroke Pines, FL: R. Klotz, 1990.

Kramer, Sydelle, and Jenny Masur, eds. *Jewish Grandmothers*. Boston: Beacon Press, 1976.

Lagemann, Ellen Condliffe. *A Generation of Women: Education in the Lives of Progressive Reformers*. Cambridge: Harvard University Press, 1979.

McCourt, Frank. *Angela's Ashes*. New York: Scribner, 1996.

———. *'Tis: A Memoir*. New York: Scribner, 1999.

Pavel, Anya (pseudonym). In *Line Five: The Internal Passport*, ed. Elaine Pomper Snyderman and Margaret Thomas Witknosky, 272–276. Chicago: Chicago Review Press, 1992.

Polacheck, Hilda Satt. *I Came a Stranger*. Urbana: University of Illinois Press, 1989.

Prikopa, Maria Lucik. *If I Told You Everything This Would Be a Book*. Chicago: John Ivan Prikopa, 1912.

Reid, Robert L., ed. *Battleground: The Autobiography of Margaret A. Haley*. Urbana: University of Illinois, 1982.

Rosen, Sara. *My Lost World: A Survivors Tale*. Portland, OR: Vallentine Mitchell, 1993.

Rubin, Stevin J., ed. *Writing Our Lives: Autobiographies of American Jews, 1890–1990*. Philadelphia: Jewish Publication Society, 1991.

Schwartz, Bessie. "My Own Story." In *The East European Jewish Experience in America*, ed. Uri D. Herscher, 153–175. Cincinnati: American Jewish Archives, 1983.

Soyer, Daniel. "The Voices of Jewish Immigrant Mothers in the Yivo American Jewish Autobiography Collection." *Journal of American Ethnic History* 17 (1998): 87–94.

Umantsev, Julia Zissman. "A Reduction of Remedies. "In *Line Five. The Internal Passport*, ed. Elaine Pomper Snyderman and Margaret Thomas Witknosky, 102–09. Chicago: Chicago Review Press, 1992.

Wald, Lillian. "Crowded Districts." In *The East European Jewish Experience in America*, ed. Uri D. Herscher, 125–135. Cincinnati: American Jewish Archives, 1983.

White, Richard. *Remembering Ahanagran*. New York: Hill and Wang, 1998.

Newspapers

Austin News
Chicago Tribune
The Green and White

Documents

The American-Irish Historical Society. Annual Address of the President General Edward A. Moseley, February 17, 1898. Hotel Reno, New York.

Chicago Board of Education. A Year of Americanization Work, July 1918–July 1919. Chicago, Illinois.

Chicago Board of Education. Annual Reports, 1900–1959. Chicago, Illinois.

Chicago Board of Education. Annual Report of the General Superintendent of the Chicago Public Schools, 1900–1959. Chicago, Illinois.

Chicago Board of Education. Annual Report of the Superintendent of Compulsory Education for the School Year Ending June 29, 1923.

Chicago Board of Education. Annual Report of the Superintendent of Compulsory Education Showing the Work of the Bureau of Compulsory Education During 1937–1938. Chicago, Illinois.

Chicago Board of Education. Education for Citizenship, March 1933. Chicago, Illinois.

Chicago Board of Education. Proceedings, 1900–1959. Chicago, Illinois.

Chicago Board of Education. School Census of the City of Chicago, 1908, 1910, 1914. Chicago, Illinois.

Degler, Carl N. "Is There a History of Women?" An inaugural lecture delivered before Oxford University on 14 March 1974. Oxford: Oxford University Press, 1975.

Gonzalez, Josue M., and Linda Darling-Hammond. *New Concepts for New Challenges: Professional Development for Teachers of Immigrant Youth.* Center for Applied Linguistics, Washington, D.C., Delta Systems Inc., McHenry, IL, 1997, ERIC, ED 421 018.

Intercultural Development Research Association. *Educating Recent Immigrants.* Reprint of *IDRA Newsletter* 21 (1994), ERIC, ED 366492.

Loomis, Frank D. *Americanization in Chicago. The Report of a Survey.* Chicago: Chicago Community Trust, 1920.

Sanders, Irwin T., and Ewa T. Morawska. *Polish-American Community Life: A Survey of Research.* Boston: Community Sociology Training Program, Department of Sociology, Boston University and Polish Institute of Arts and Sciences in America, Inc., June 1975.

U.S. Congress. 61st Congress, Senate, 3rd Session, 1910, Reports of the Immigration Commission, *The Children of Immigrants in Schools*, vol. 2. Metuchen, NJ: Scarecrow Reprint Corporation, 1970.

U.S. Department of Education. U.S. Department of Education Fiscal Year 1999 Annual Plan, vol. 2: Program Performance Plans. Washington, D.C., 1999. ERIC, ED 417911.

U.S. Department of Education. Department of Education Fiscal Year 1999. Budget: Summary and Background Information. Washington, D.C., 1999. ERIC, ED 415 576.

Unpublished Theses and Dissertations

Edson, Christopher Howard. "Immigrant Perspectives on Work and Schooling: Eastern European Jews and Southern Italians, 1880–1920." Ph.D. dissertation, Stanford University, 1979.

Kowalenko, Empaster's thesis, Northeastern Illinois University, 1984.

McCarthy, Joseph J. "History of Black Catholic Education in Chicago 1871–
1971." Ph.D. dissertation, Loyola University, 1973.

Parot, Joseph. "The American Faith and the Persistence of Chicago Polonia,
1870–1920." Ph.D. dissertation, Northern Illinois University, 1971.

Writh, Louis. "Culture Conflicts in the Immigrant Family." Master's thesis,
University of Chicago, 1925.

Manuscript Collections

Austin High School Collection. Harold Washington Library, Special Collections and Preservation Department, Chicago, Illinois.

Englewood High School Collection. Harold Washington Library, Special
Collections and Preservation Department, Chicago, Illinois.

Immigrant Protective League. University of Illinois at Chicago, University
Library, Special Collections Department, Chicago, Illinois.

Italian American Oral History Project. University of Illinois at Chicago,
University Library, Special Collections Department, Chicago, Illinois.

Oral History Archives of Chicago Polonia. Chicago Historical Society,
Archives and Manuscripts Department, Chicago, Illinois.

Scholarship and Guidance Association. University of Illinois at Chicago,
University Library, Special Collections Department, Chicago, Illinois.

United Charities. Chicago Historical Society, Archives and Manuscripts
Department, Chicago, Illinois.

HISTORY OF
SCHOOLS &
SCHOOLING

THIS SERIES EXPLORES THE HISTORY OF SCHOOLS AND SCHOOLING in the United States and other countries. Books in this series examine the historical development of schools and educational processes, with special emphasis on issues of educational policy, curriculum and pedagogy, as well as issues relating to race, class, gender, and ethnicity. Special emphasis will be placed on the lessons to be learned from the past for contemporary educational reform and policy. Although the series will publish books related to education in the broadest societal and cultural context, it especially seeks books on the history of specific schools and on the lives of educational leaders and school founders.

For additional information about this series or for the submission of manuscripts, please contact the general editors:

Alan R. Sadovnik   Susan F. Semel
Rutgers University-Newark   The City College of New York, CUNY
Education Dept.   138th Street and Convent Avenue
155 Conklin Hall   NAC 5/208
175 University Avenue   New York, NY 10031
Newark, NJ 07102

To order other books in this series, please contact our Customer Service Department:

800-770-LANG (within the U.S.)
212-647-7706 (outside the U.S.)
212-647-7707 FAX

Or browse online by series at:

www.peterlangusa.com